FACING DAWN
A Morning Devotional for the Brokenhearted

By
Tammy Nischan

D1530867

In Memory of.........

Adrienne Annabeth Nischan

In six short weeks she taught us more about the meaning of life than volumes of books ever could.

Nicholas Yancy Nischan

In 13 years he gained the wisdom of a saint and graciously shared some of it with us.

I love and miss you both every single day.
My heart now beats for all three of us and for that I am thankful.

Zachary Charles Yoho

Although I never had the pleasure of meeting him before he passed away, I feel as if I know him well. Through my friendship with his mom and dad, I have grown to love his smiling face. I look forward to getting to know him in Heaven.

Table of Contents

Dedication

This book never would have happened had it not been for so many friends and family members pushing me along the way.

First, thank you, Tim, for being my 24/7 coach, friend, encourager, and attitude adjuster. You taught me to see the glass half full, and I am forever thankful. Twenty-seven years ago you gave me the book, "Introduction to Christian Writing." You saw a writer in me before I had anything to write about.

Thank you Erich, Evan, Todd, and Olivia, for allowing me to pen our family's life through my blog even when I mentioned things like your habit of not wearing your retainers faithfully. Your permission for me to write freely has allowed me to be transparent and honest. My life is complete because of you.

Evan, you especially lit a writer's fire in me more than once as you saw me slipping away from my dream. Thank you for holding me accountable and not giving up on me. Every book I write from this day forward will be written because you pushed me uphill when I was sliding down.

Cynde, for over twenty years you tried to convince me to write. I told you a long time ago that if I ever published a book, it would be dedicated to you; because you, too, saw a writer in me before I ever believed there was one. Please know none of these words would be on paper if it weren't for your constant encouragement over the years.

Mom and Dad, I've read a lot about the temperament of a writer, and it's made me feel a little better about the moody girl you raised. Thank you for loving me through my ugly years and for sticking with me through my painful ones. I love you both so much!

Janet, our friendship is bittersweet. We became friends through our deep grief, but I believe we have remained friends because of our deep faith in an eternal Home where our children await us! As I wrote the reflection sections of this book, I had your precious face in my mind. I love you more than you'll ever know. I love your husband, Wes, and I love your son, Zach, who I look forward to meeting and hugging when I cross over to the other side! Oh, what a day that will be!! Thank you for being my kindred-spirited sister in the Lord. I am honored to share life with you!

Georgia, you have counseled me so many times and encouraged me as a writer. I've learned so much from your example! Thank you for believing in me!

Terry Whalin, even though this book is releasing without your name attached to it in any official way, I couldn't possibly publish this without adding your name. As an author, publisher, and speaker, you have continued to encourage me to get this first book finished, so that I can move on to write more. Your random and unexpected phone calls always reignite my passion and help me remember that my words matter. Your tears as you shared of your own grief will never be forgotten. I am thankful for you, and I hope we work on a project together soon!

Donnette, Donna, Mallory, Cindy, Martha, Tiffany, Sherry, Topsy, Vicki, Gina, Pam, Brenda, Linda, Sandra, Abby, Jennie, Barbara, Melanie, Laurie, Christine, Barbara, Becky, Robin, Elaina, Renee, Glynnis, Lysa, Marybeth, Melissa, Angie, Trish, Lesa, Robin, Clara, Jackie, Sherry, Margo, Kristy, Becky, Kim, Brooke, Roxy, Brooke, Amy, Carol, Lee, Charlotte, Tracy, Patti, and the list goes on and on.........
Thank you for being my friends and for loving me through so many ups and downs in life. Where would I be without each of you? I don't even want to imagine!

In many ways, I'm not a writer.
I'm just a grieving mom, trying to find peace with God.
I just happen to use words as I search.

Through my writing, I have finally found peace.

How can I ever thank you enough for the part you have played in my journey?

Preface

There's no easy way to wake up with grief.

Every sunrise brings with it a fresh reminder of the sadness deep inside your soul, as if the awareness of your pain and loss are entering your heart and mind for the very first time all over again. Regrets, questions, doubts, and bittersweet memories seem to well up inside you almost as quickly as your room fills with the morning light.

In my early grief after losing my daughter, the first hours of every morning were the most difficult part of my day. Morning seemed to whisper cruel thoughts as my chest felt the weight of what my heart could not bear. Adrienne's crib was empty. Dreams were shattered. Family pictures would never be the same. Sunlight seemed to carry with it a darkness no one around me could understand. As I chartered the unfamiliar waters of grief, dawn assaulted me with the most brutal waves of sadness.

I learned a lot in my grief as a young mom.

I learned that no one can walk you through the darkness of a broken heart.

Friends tried.

They invited me over for coffee and devotions.

They sent me cards.

They included me in events with their children.

They did everything within their power to fix me, and I'm thankful for all their acts of kindness. I'm sure that without them my journey would have been even longer and more difficult.

In spite of all their efforts, though, no one could give me what I really needed; because what I needed had been taken from me forever.

Grief is a complicated friend to walk alongside. I'm sure many of my friends became exhausted as they continued to share life with both me and my grief.

I muddled my way through many years of life, and my grief transformed into depression as time passed. Honestly, I don't think I really snapped out of my veiled and profound sadness from losing my daughter until my youngest son was diagnosed with a brain tumor. Suddenly, the present pain superseded my desire to hang on to the pain of my past. "Lord, please don't take Nick, too," became my prayer.

Six and a half years passed as Nick fought cancer, recovered, and became sick again multiple times. During those difficult but memory-filled years, God taught me how to be fully present in life again. He reminded me of just how precious every sunrise is, and He taught me how to live with a spirit of joy instead of a spirit of regret.

When Nick lost his fight with cancer in 2008 at the age of 13, I knew I couldn't survive if I grieved in the same way I had grieved as a young mom. I knew the pain of living without Nick could easily overtake me if I did not have a plan, so I began reading the Bible every single day and writing my way out of my heartache. These two decisions have made the difference between a broken, bitter life and a life filled with purpose in spite of my deep pain.

This book holds part of my journey towards finding peace in the midst of my heartache. I hope it will become part of your journey too. I have included Scriptures as well as questions for you to both reflect on and respond to as you journey through grief. I think you will find writing through your sadness a powerful step in the difficult but necessary routine of *Facing Dawn*.

The Naming of This Book

The cover photo of this book holds as much meaning in my heart as every word I penned in my journey through my early grief. I took this sunrise photograph with Nick sitting right beside me just four months before he passed away.

My friend Donnette and I had taken Nick, Todd, and one of their buddies to spend a week at the beach the summer that his prognosis became very grim, and we decided to get up early on our last morning of the trip so we could watch the sun rise over the ocean's horizon. I can remember vividly all the different emotions flowing through my heart as the sun battled the clouds just to make a partial appearance. With Nick at my side and the sound of the ocean waves lapping in, I fought back tears as I felt God speaking to my heart with every click of my camera.

It was as if He had planned all along to use this particular morning to prepare me for the dark days ahead. Every inch of my being knew that this moment in time would be my constant reminder that no matter how dark the clouds became God's Son would continue to be with our family, battling His way back into our view as we struggled to face each new and painful morning.

Several years after Nick's death, I met a beautiful young woman at a writer's conference who had recently and very unexpectedly lost her husband. As I spoke with her, she said, *"Mornings are so hard."*

I asked her if I could pray with her and then asked for her name.
She looked at me with tears in her eyes and said, "Dawn."
As I began to pray, I realized that I was *facing Dawn* who was struggling to do just that every morning of her life.

God used this precious memory along with my last sunrise with Nick to inspire the title for this book.

I hope your journey through this book will help you ***Face Dawn*** with a sense of peace, hope, and joy that causes you to celebrate the life of the one for whom you are grieving.

I hope you will never forget that you are never alone as you wake to face the next dawn.

Because of the LORD's great love we are not consumed, for his compassions never fail.
They are new every morning;
great is your faithfulness. (NIV)

Lamentations 3:22-23

FACING DAWN

When Your Mind is Spinning

Isaiah 26:3
You will keep in perfect peace
him whose mind is steadfast,
because he trusts in you. (NIV)

Grief has a way of taking over my mind..............

Sometimes grief overtakes me so strongly that even words
are hard to string together into sentences.

Thoughts swirl.............

Good memories
Sad memories
Feelings of confusion
Feelings of anger
Feelings of loneliness
Questions with no answers

When I step away from my thoughts, I can almost see them
swirling beside me. As I watch them spin uncontrollably, I
realize other things have created their own little "cyclones of
pain" in our family's world of grief,

Evan's heart
Erich's heart
Todd's heart

Olivia's heart
Tim's heart
My mom's heart
My friends' hearts

We're all hurting, all unsure of how to regroup or what to say, all broken in different ways........

Grief is not a simple emotion we face for a short season and then quietly push away.

It is complex and long-lasting.

I know, because I remember.

I remember grief before this grief.

I remember losing Adrienne 16 years before losing Nick.

While I know deep inside that eventually the pain lessened and life became somewhat "normal" (a word I don't particularly like anymore) after her sudden death, right now I just can't bear the thought of life without Nick ever being easy........

That's where I'm at today.

Hurting and yet never wanting **NOT** to hurt. That probably makes no sense, but in my heart it does.

Grief consumed my weekend, making even writing my thoughts a daunting task. Writing releases part of my heartache, though, so I'm forcing myself today. Because when I write, I somehow pull myself out of my own cyclone, and I'm finally able to think clearly again for a while.

It's almost as if the devil pushes me down and stands on my chest in some sort of victory stance from time to time, and I have to somehow figure out a way to push him off and stand back up again.

The devil loves grief, I am sure. He loves its power to immobilize and anger God's people.

At the same time, I know God loves it too, because it drives me back to Him time and time again.....in spite of my questions and my sadness........

Only through writing am I able to overcome the devil's attempt to overcome me.

When I write down all the thoughts that are spinning in my mind, I provide a space for God to come and calm me......a space for God's grace and presence.

When I feel His presence, joy begins to seep back into my heart.

I'm giving God my spinning thoughts today and searching for joy at the same time, knowing somehow God will provide just what I need. I know He'll provide what you need to.

REFLECTION TIME:

Does your mind ever swirl with too many thoughts? Many times when this happens it is easy to be overcome with such deep feelings of sadness that moving on to the "next thing" in the day seems impossible. Jot down everything that is spinning around in your head. Ask God to help you take all these thoughts and give them to Him. He longs to calm your heart and mind and bring a sense of peace and joy even in your heartache.

_____

_____

_____

_____

_____

_____

_____

_____

_____

_____

_____

_____

_____

When You're Scared

Psalm 56:3-4
When I am afraid,
I will trust in you.
In God, whose word I praise,
in God I trust; I will not be afraid.
What can mortal man do to me?

Our phone rang late tonight..........

An elderly lady from our church family asked if my husband could stop by to see her brother (who lives with her) sometime soon.

He has cancer, and he is scared.

Tim came to the phone to pray because they didn't want him driving at that hour of the night.

Fear –

It grabs us, consumes us, and often controls us.

I can remember so many days and nights of feeling fearful as Nick faced medical tests, new treatments, frequent pain, and oh, so many needles.

One day a friend shared Psalm 56:3-4 with me, and it became one of my strongholds throughout Nick's fight with cancer. I continue to cling to it in my grief. This verse kept me from drowning in my fear time after time.

This Psalm brought comfort when nothing else could. It reminded me over and over again that clinging to God's Word was truly my only HOPE!

It reminded me that NO MATTER WHAT this world throws my way, I cannot be overtaken when God is on my side. And neither could Nick.

So, tonight, as I head to bed-

Another day of life soaked up with heartache, yes, but laughter too.

I feel thankful.

Thankful that God keeps His promises.

Yes, that's right.

He is Faithful.

Faithful to provide just what I need when I need it most.

And faithful to provide just what you need too.

REFLECTION TIME:

Fear is a very normal feeling when you are dealing with loss. What are you afraid of today? Take a minute to write down a few things that scare you and then read Psalm 56:3-4 out loud and claim it as God's promise to you today.

_____

_____

_____

_____

_____

_____

_____

_____

_____

_____

_____

_____

_____

_____

When Life Seems Empty

I John 1:1-4
That which was from the beginning, which we have heard,
which we have seen with our eyes, which we have looked at
and our hands have touched—this we proclaim concerning
the Word of life. The life appeared; we have seen it and
testify to it, and we proclaim to you the eternal life, which
was with the Father and has appeared to us. We proclaim to
you what we have seen and heard, so that you also may
have fellowship with us. And our fellowship is with the
Father and with his Son, Jesus Christ.
We write this to make our joy complete.

I remember after we lost Adrienne, I struggled for a long, long time with how to use my time. I had been so busy with two little boys and a brand new baby girl. My days, once packed with changing diapers, nursing Adrienne, taking walks, playing with the boys, and so many other "mommy" things, were now void of many joyous things.

Suddenly, her crib was empty. My arms ached to hold my chubby little baby. Erich and Evan couldn't understand why Adrienne couldn't come back. The boys would say things out of the blue that caused my heart to break all over again.

I remember Evan, who was only two at the time, would often say, "Feed Adjun, Mommy," like he couldn't understand how Adrienne was okay without me taking care of her every need.

Our days changed from walks around the neighborhood to walks through the cemetery.

Our afternoons changed from going to a friend's house for play time to going to a friend's house simply so the boys could be entertained while I worked through my sadness.

I don't think I really started to "pull out" of my grief until I started noticing others who were hurting.

It wasn't until I started encouraging others that I began to feel encouraged.

I bought stationery and began sending notes to friends; and in those notes, I began to find some kind of strength and joy.

I had forgotten about this part of my first journey through grief as a mom who lost a child, until the other day. I was digging through some old papers to work on a class project, and a note fell to the floor. I had received this note almost five years ago, and somehow it had been placed in one of my graduate school notebooks.....for such a time as this.

As I read the note for the first time in years, so many memories came back to me from a different time in my life.

Memories of a different season when I had different struggles.

Memories of a friend who has now moved to Michigan.

Memories of a simpler time in my life as a wife and mom.

As I read the note, I realized how powerful encouraging words can be, and I knew that God was calling me to reach outside of my own pain and begin encouraging others.

He gently reminded me of the significance of a simple hand-written note.

Words transcend time and, once written, can be used again and again to minister and share love.

I love 1 John 1:1-4 not only because the writer longs to share the power of the resurrection and the hope of eternal life, but also because he says that "we write so that OUR joy may be complete!"

Not just the joy of the reader.

But also the joy of the writer!

REFLECTION TIME:
Make a list of friends who are struggling. Say a prayer for them: Then send them a note of love and encouragement. Through the note you will not only brighten a friend's day but also brighten your own!
Looking for my stationery and hoping you are too!

_____

_____

_____

_____

_____

_____

_____

_____

_____

_____

_____

_____

_____

When Your Thoughts Are Dark

I truly don't know how people walk the road of grief without
the hope of Heaven.

I am struggling......even while I have this hope.

I can't imagine where I'd be without it.

Christ says,

"Let anyone who is thirst come to me and drink."
John 7:37
*"I am the light of the world. Whoever follows me will never
walk in darkness, but will have the light of life."*
John 8:12
"If you hold to my teaching, you are really my disciples."
John 8:31

And regarding a man blind from birth, Jesus says,

*"Neither this man nor his parents sinned," said Jesus, "but
this happened so that the work of God might be displayed in
his life."*
John 9:3-4

I believe these words....all of them.

I really do.

But somehow grief, like some sort of monster, plays games with my mind.

I feel parched spiritually even though I stay deep in the Word.

I feel darkness around me even though I strive to stay in the light.

I do not feel like one of Jesus' disciples even though I love Him more than I love anyone else in this world.

I feel guilty even though I KNOW I did not cause Nick to be sick.

Oh, grief.

You are cruel.

So, I look to II Corinthians 10:4-5,

"The weapons we fight with are not the weapons of the world. On the contrary, they have divine power to demolish strongholds. We demolish arguments and every pretension that sets itself up against the knowledge of God, and we take captive every thought to make it obedient to Christ."

I keep praying this passage back to God.

Lord, demolish all arguments that set themselves up against Your knowledge.

*Take all of my thoughts **captive** and make them obedient to Your Son.*

Captive.

Lord, I long to take all my grief-driven thoughts captive. Put them behind bars. Lock them up for life.

I know because of the evil in this world and the somewhat limited and yet often effective power of the devil, the bars will be loosened time and time again..........

Freeing my thoughts to wander, scramble, and stray.

So, my prayer this morning is that every time I feel the door swinging open, I will become more and more equipped to shut it quickly and bravely.

REFLECTION TIME:

Is your mind wandering to dark thoughts? Do you feel discouraged in your grief? Are you questioning God's presence in your pain? Tell Him all about it and then claim II Corinthians 10:4-5 as one of your new life passages.

_____

_____

_____

_____

_____

_____

_____

_____

_____

_____

_____

_____

_____

FACING DAWN

With a Heavy Heart

Matt. 11:28
Come to me, all you who are weary and burdened, and I will
give you rest.

Shew.

That seems to be the first word out of my mouth lately.......

Or the first word in my texts to friends..........

Or the first word I type in emails.............

Shew.

I'm just taking deep breaths in and deep breaths out.

Sometimes the simplest tasks become the most difficult tasks
when you are walking the road of grief.

Packing is one of those simple tasks that now seems nearly
impossible.

We decided staying home for Christmas would be too
painful. There are too many traditions that Nick loved and
looked forward to that we are forced to face if we stay home.

So, my husband and I, along with Erich, Evan, Todd, and Olivia (our four other children), are leaving at 4 a.m. for an 18-hour drive to Oklahoma to visit my grandpa, aunt, and cousins.

My parents, who live "on the way", are meeting us at an exit a few hours from here and traveling along with us in their car.

We will be driving 13 hours tomorrow and spending three nights in Branson, Missouri, on the way to the panhandle of Oklahoma.

On Christmas Eve we will drive 6 more hours and arrive in time to spend the evening with family in Beaver, Oklahoma.

Shew.

So many miles to drive, so much to do before we leave, and here I sit.

I had to stop long enough to say, "Packing is so difficult when you're grieving."

I miss Nick so much and not packing for him has been extremely painful. He loved trips. He would have been right here beside me, reminding me of things we needed, asking if I needed help. He was just that kind of kid.

And walking through his room, I long to stop and help him pick out jammies, video games, and other things he would definitely want to bring along.

Tonight has been a night of tears. I took a bath and cried. I thought I had regrouped when my mom called to remind me of something I needed to bring, and I found myself losing it on the phone with her.

Shew.

Oh, Nick, I miss you so much. I miss your great big smile and gentle spirit. I miss your hugs. I miss your sweet hand rubbing my back as I walk by you.

In the midst of my sadness tonight, I came across a burned CD that Nick had "humbly" titled, "Nick's Amazingly Awesome Music CD." I put it in the CD player in the kitchen and was immediately reminded of what a fun boy Nick was!

Thank you, God, for continuing to remind me of what a great blessing Nick was and will continue to be in my life. Thank you for bringing a smile from Nick even in his absence. Thank you for the hope of Heaven!

REFLECTION TIME:

In our sadness and pain, it is often difficult to say "thank you" for the memories we share with the one we are missing. Sometimes though, even if it causes us to cry, it is therapeutic to write down memories and reflect on the joy we shared in those precious moments. Take a few minutes to write about a couple of your special memories and then tell how these memories cause you to say, "Thank you, Lord," for the life you shared with your loved one.

_____

_____

_____

_____

_____

_____

_____

_____

_____

_____

_____

_____

On Christmas Day

Our first Christmas Day without Nick came and went.

The reality of Nick's absence rang in my ears constantly-
sometimes like a clanging cymbal, other times like the light
ringing of a gentle chime.

We took our first family picture without Nick in Aunt
Earlene's back yard on Christmas Day.

I can't believe I'm writing those words: Our first "family
picture" without Nick.

I'm sure I'll never get use to looking at a picture of our family without his radiant smile in the midst of us.

I can't help but think that somewhere among the branches he is grinning and sharing this moment with us. I know he was smiling in my heart.

I think he was smiling because we were trying to make Christmas Day special even though our hearts were broken.

I've asked myself often, "What should I do on holidays when my heart is so heavy and sad?"

I feel like God keeps whispering the same words into my heart every time the question surfaces. It's as if I can imagine Him saying, "Embrace the day."

Embrace the day? Really? But then I think, "What else can I do when I have the hope of Heaven set before me?"

If Nick could have made the choice of spending the day with us climbing an old tree to say "cheese" or spending the day in the presence of the One for whom we celebrate the holiday, I just have to believe he would have chosen praising Jesus.

So, as Nick's mom, I have to honor my son by choosing to spend God's Son's birthday praising Him as well! Nick would have wanted nothing less from our family.

We made it through Christmas, and we are thankful and relieved.

No matter how painful your loss, I know you can make it too.

REFLECTION TIME:

What Christmas memories do you miss the most in your grief? Write about some of them. Share some things that you do or would like to do in the future to make the holidays easier? Think about how you could make these thoughts a reality.

_____

_____

_____

_____

_____

_____

_____

_____

_____

_____

_____

_____

_____

When Part of Your Life is Missing

For now we see only a reflection as in a mirror; then we shall see face to face. Now I know in part; then I shall know fully, even as I am fully known.
I Corinthians 13:12

Todd and his friend Caleb have spent the last couple of nights putting together this puzzle.

Since Todd received a new camera for Christmas, he has been taking pictures of everything!

Thankfully, he took a picture of this puzzle from time to time along the way! When I was looking through his photos and saw this one, it spoke to me in such a powerful way.

Especially when I saw the "accidental" heart right in the middle!

I couldn't help but think of I Corinthians 13 when it says that now we "see through a glass darkly" and then goes on to promise that one day we will know fully just as we are fully known.

Oh, for that day!

Oh, to see how each piece of our life fits together to make God's masterpiece.

Oh, to understand that sometimes it is in the missing pieces that God can form a perfect heart!

Tonight as I watch 2008 end and prepare for 2009.............

My first year without Nick and my seventeenth year without Adrienne.........

I am praying that God will keep my heart focused on His masterpiece and not on my missing pieces.

I am praying that I will remember that until that day when my faith becomes sight, I will not be able to see the "whole picture."

But when I do............

Oh, what a glorious day that will be!

REFLECTION TIME:
What parts of your life feel like missing puzzle pieces?
When you think of God as a "Masterpiece Creator" what
does that say to you about your future? One day, we will see
the finished puzzle. All our longings and heartache will be
washed away in the presence of Him. What do you look
forward to most about that day?

_____

_____

_____

_____

_____

_____

_____

_____

_____

_____

_____

_____

_____

_____

When You Are Weary

But whatever was to my profit I now consider loss for the sake of Christ. What is more, I consider everything a loss compared to the surpassing greatness of knowing Christ Jesus my Lord, for whose sake I have lost all things. I consider them rubbish, that I may gain Christ and be found in him, not having a righteousness of my own that comes from the law, but that which is through faith in Christ—the righteousness that comes from God and is by faith. Not that I have already obtained all this, or have already been made perfect, but I press on to take hold of that for which Christ Jesus took hold of me. Brothers, I do not consider myself yet to have taken hold of it. But one thing I do: Forgetting what is behind and straining toward what is ahead, I press on toward the goal to win the prize for which God has called me heavenward in Christ Jesus......

.......but our citizenship is in heaven. And we eagerly await a Savior from there, the Lord Jesus Christ.

Phil 3:7-12, 14

As much as I love this passage, as much as the passage inspires me to keep on keeping on, I find myself fighting these verses tooth and nail.

I struggle to grasp what God is asking of me.

I struggle to make sense of His Words.

I struggle with the passage above, because when I think of Nick and Adrienne, I don't want to forget what is behind me.

I can't.

They were, are, and always will be a part of who I am.

And honestly, the loss of Nick has shoved me back to the death of Adrienne like a bulldozer moving dirt. I think I had tucked away the pain of losing my baby girl as we tried to "move on" with life when God gave us Todd, then Nick, and then the adoption of Olivia. I always believed that Adrienne was waiting for me in Heaven, so I developed a level of peace over the years since she went Home.

Life had become busy with five kids and a teaching career. While I continued to change the flowers on her grave every season, year in and year out, while looking forward to the day when we would be reunited, I had somehow suppressed my grief.

So when Nick was first diagnosed with a brain tumor at the age of seven, I remember crying out to God, "Please, no! Please don't take another child from me."

Suddenly the loss of Adrienne was overshadowed by the struggle to keep Nick alive.

Tonight I sit here facing the reality that two of my children have gone Home before me.

So, I read the verse about "forgetting what is behind," and I want to scream, "HOW?! WHY?! WHAT ARE YOU ASKING OF ME?!?!?"

I think I am just now beginning to wrap my mind around the depth of what the verses above are saying.

I believe it's not so much about "forgetting" what's behind as it is about "dwelling" on it.

In a race, the victor is generally the one who keeps his eye on the finish line. He is not constantly glancing back to see who or what is about to overtake him. He is focused on winning, on reaching his goal.

That's the kind of spiritual runner I want to be.

Not one who forgets I am in a race.

Not one who forgets the aspects of my race that have made me the runner that I am.

But one who takes the hurdles as they come, staying focused on the finish line.

I will never forget Nick.

I will never forget Adrienne.

They are a part of me that can never be taken away.

They are the strength in my legs as I keep pressing forward.

I hear a whisper from somewhere in my heart, reminding me that pressing on doesn't mean forgetting, as I think of this truth, "God doesn't ask us to forget His Son." In fact, He calls us to remembrance of Him and His crucifixion every Sunday morning as we gather around the Lord's Table to break bread. God says, "Do this in remembrance of Him....of me."

Comfort engulfs me as I realize that just as I am created in the image of my Creator, my longing to remember my children comes from Him who also longs for me to remember His Child.

Thank you, Heavenly Father, for modeling healthy remembrance.

As I remember my precious children, I must also stay focused on the finish line, straining toward what is ahead. I cannot sit down on the track when the race seems too difficult. I cannot throw in the towel.

I believe that is why Paul wrote these verses in Philippians. He wasn't telling us to forget everything from our past. He was encouraging us not to get bogged down to the point of becoming unable to finish our race victoriously. He knew that one of the devil's schemes is to keep us so broken from this world's pain that the thought of finishing the race seems daunting, even impossible. I cannot let the devil win.

Oh, believe me! I am in a spiritual battle.

My legs are weary. My feet ache.

How do I handle this spiritual fatigue from grief while trying to remain strong in my life race?

I cling to more and more promises from God's Word.

I remember, "Those who wait upon the Lord shall renew their strength."
Is. 40:31

I remember that Christ says, "*In this world you will have trouble, but take heart! I have overcome the world.*"
John 16:33

If the race of life has you feeling weary and you find yourself losing sight of the finish line, I encourage you to search God's Word for promises that remind you of His presence even on the toughest days.

I Thess. 5:11 says, "*We must encourage one another and build each other up...*"

I want to encourage you to keep your eye on the prize!!!!

The race of life is not easy, but the prize will be worth every drop of sweat, every tear!!!

Face dawn and press on!

REFLECTION TIME:
Do you feel tired today? Are you weary? What would it take to re-energize you and help you feel an extra burst of energy in order to press on toward the finish line? Tell God how you feel. Ask Him for what you need. Then trust Him to deliver.

_____

_____

_____

_____

_____

_____

_____

_____

_____

_____

_____

_____

_____

_____

When Something's Empty

"The Empty Chair"

I long to see you sitting there
 I glance from time to time
The reality of your absence
 Is always on my mind

Sometimes Olivia plops right down
 And shares a minute or two
Snoopy sleeps there often
 As if that will be your cue

To walk in and say, "Get up, girl,
 and give me back my seat,"
But then I quickly realize
 As my heart seems to skip a beat-

That even your voice is missing
 From our home but not our heart
The memory of your smile
 Will never from us part.

Oh, Nick, we love you so much
 You taught us more than any degree
Your chair may lack your presence
 But it's never really empty

Cause your spirit's in the chair-
I know it really is!

You still keep us on our toes
Every action, every word we say
From your memory flows-

Thank you, Nick, for leading the way
With your courage and your love
We'll live for Him until the day
We meet you up above!

See you soon.

Love, Your Mommy

REFLECTION TIME:

When we lose someone we love, we notice their absence in all sorts of different ways - empty chairs, empty beds, empty swings, empty homes, and on and on. What is empty in your life because of your loss? Write a poem about this empty place. You'll be surprised how God fills that empty place with special memories to cherish forever in your heart.

FACING DAWN

When You Are Feeling Fragile

Therefore I will boast all the more gladly about my weaknesses, so that Christ's power may rest on me. That is why, for Christ's sake, I delight in weaknesses, in insults, in hardships, in persecutions, in difficulties. For when I am weak, then I am strong.
2 Corinthians 12:9-10

I took this picture of my Aunt Earlene's "Kitchen Christmas Tree," laden with dainty tea cups.

I could look at this tree for hours from every different angle and never stop finding new and fascinating dishes!

As I looked through my pictures of this special tree after we returned home, my eyes were drawn to this particular tea cup and plate hanging precariously from a branch. I couldn't help but feel a kindred spirit stir within me as I saw reflected in this cup an image of myself.

Fragile.

Easily broken.

Hanging on to the last limb.

Grief reaches down into my soul and tugs at every emotion, every nerve-ending, every insecurity, every doubt.....

Grief then places all of these sensitive aspects of my being on display for the world to see.

This exposing of my weaknesses causes me to feel very frail.

Words said by others, in love or without thinking, can cut my heart like a knife - words that in the past I would have forgotten moments later.

Actions of even the closest friends can leave me wondering if they really care. I know they really do, but my heart has no room for new pain, even if it is unintentional.

It's strange but when you're grieving, it's almost as if God calls you to a higher level of grace and mercy.

I've often tried to place someone else in my shoes and thought, "What would I say? How would I act?"

The truth is...........

I don't know.

There is often no right way to please or comfort a grieving friend other than just being there to listen.

Sharing Scriptures............maybe.

Sending a text just to say, "I love you."

Watching a movie together.

Something safe.

CS Lewis, in his book <u>A Grief Observed</u>, said he became angry when people asked about his wife who had recently passed away, and he became angry when they didn't. I totally understand what he was saying.

If you're grieving and feeling frail, I'm praying you can develop a level of grace and mercy with your friends and family. They love you. They are sad with you. They just feel helpless and in moments of feeling wordless, they often speak without thinking.

Grief is a journey that has to be traveled to a certain extent..............alone.............with God.

If you find yourself being easily hurt by your friends' words or actions, remember this: right now you are like a dainty tea cup hanging from a lone branch. Sometimes you are going to get chipped accidentally.

You are fragile.

There's good news, though!

God's power can be made perfect through us if we turn to Him for strength. Listen to what He said to Paul when Paul pleaded for help,

"My grace is sufficient for you, for my power is made perfect in weakness."

If you long to feel the perfect power of God working inside you, remember that He works best when you are weak. Today, even though you're feeling frail, lean back in God's arms and experience the same delight Paul did when He penned these words,

Therefore I will boast all the more gladly about my weaknesses, so that Christ's power may rest on me. That is why, for Christ's sake, I delight in weaknesses, in insults, in hardships, in persecutions, in difficulties. For when I am weak, then I am strong.

2 Corinthians 12:9-10

REFLECTION TIME:

In what ways have you felt frail lately? How could God use
your weakness to make you strong?
Who do you know that may also be feeling weak these days?
How could you encourage them?

_____

_____

_____

_____

_____

_____

_____

_____

_____

_____

_____

_____

_____

FACING DAWN

When You Feel Broken

II Corinthians 4:7-9
But we have this treasure in jars of clay to show that this all-surpassing power is from God and not from us.
We are hard pressed on every side, but not crushed;
perplexed, but not in despair; persecuted, but not abandoned; struck down, but not destroyed.

Ever since Nick passed away, our main living room has been nothing more than a storage room and dark passageway from our bedrooms to the kitchen.

I've noticed that the room is rarely used, and the light stays off most of the time. We continue to store "Basket of Hope" items, "Adrienne's Angel" items, and all kinds of things from Nick's foundation in this room as if it has become a gigantic storage closet.

I have been bothered lately by the reality that this room is so uninviting, so dark, so "not what I want our life to be."

I knew that this weekend Erich and Evan will be moving back home from college along with three other college guys for the entire month of May................YIKES!!!!!!!!!!!!!!

So, yesterday afternoon I felt the urge to reconstruct our downstairs into a living space that felt welcoming.

At first I was overwhelmed as I looked at my kitchen, little dining area, and living room. I began pulling furniture from everywhere, so that I could have empty places to begin my work. I started dumping stacks of books and papers into laundry baskets just to get them out of my way.

As I was working, I whispered a prayer that God would somehow speak to me - show me His presence even in my rearranging of furniture. Let me know He was with me and that what I was doing was ok.

I kept moving things, thinking of the right place for little tables, my desk, lamps, etc., when suddenly from the living room I heard a very loud sound of shattering glass. My heart sank. What had fallen?

I discovered that I had left the large rectangular, very thick glass top to my dresser propped between two pieces of furniture in a not-so-secure way. Slowly, it had lost its balance, slamming down onto the brick of our fireplace.

The thick glass had shattered. Large pieces, medium-sized pieces, small pieces, and hundreds of glass specks covered the floor.
My first thought was, "WHY WAS I SO CARELESS?!?!?!?!??!?"

My second thought was, "THE LAST THING I WANT TO DO RIGHT NOW IS CLEAN UP AN UNNECESSARY MESS!!!!!!!!!!"

My third thought was, "WAIT A MINUTE............GOD JUST SHOWED UP!!"

As I knelt down to look at the mess, a tiny piece of glass pierced my knee. I pulled it out and carefully knelt again. As I surveyed the shattered glass, I saw myself in the mess. A broken person. Sharp, fragmented pieces of my heart spread out across my living room floor. The reality began to sink in as my knee ached, "In my brokenness I had become "bigger" than I was before." My broken heart had reached out to places it never would have reached in my wholeness, and this struck me as something only God could do.

Then I remembered a conversation from just an hour or so before with a dear friend of mine's mom who recently lost her husband to cancer. We had visited for about an hour and had such a wonderful talk. I had felt so revived by our conversation, so determined to take my pain and help others......and God was showing me through the broken glass that only He can take something that seems so unnecessary, so disappointing, and transform it into a message of Hope.....that spreads further than we could ever imagine.

I also remembered a part of our conversation where we had discussed the fact that Christians can sometimes be the most hurtful (unintentionally) with their words of encouragement by sharing a "verse or thought" that seems helpful but truthfully stabs a hurting heart.

"God knows best, God has a plan, God will bring good from this, and on and on."

These kinds of words, like broken glass, often cut deeper than silence.

As I stared at the pile of rubble in front of me, I began to see the shattered glass as a multitude of hurting people. Some leaning on others for strength, some trying to stand alone, some hiding so as not to be noticed (like the glass that had somehow slid under my couch),

some shattered, some leaning on the Word (like the large piece of glass that did not break because it landed on my Bible commentary! WOW!)

I realized that all of these broken pieces had one thing in common. They had sharp edges....edges that if used improperly could inflict pain.

And I realized that in my brokenness, I must be determined not to allow my sharp, hurting edges to be instruments of bitterness, judgment, and anger.

I began to take the pieces one by one and place them in a box I could tape closed (Mom always told me to remember that the garbage man would not be expecting broken glass in my trash can, so sharp objects need to be wrapped carefully.)

As I picked up each piece, I imagined friends with broken hearts. I saw my church that is full of hurting people. I saw a hurting world.

Then I picked up a piece that I knew was my "thumbs up" from God.....WOW!

This piece I saved as a reminder of the day!!!

As I swept all of the fragments together, I saw what looked like a pile of crystals...and I thought of the reality that God makes all things beautiful in His time.

Yes, God does have a plan, He does work for good, He speaks through broken things, and He does know best.....

He is able to reverse the devil's desire to shatter our dreams by using our brokenness to create something of beauty when we give our broken hearts to Him, the ultimate Healer.

REFLECTION TIME:

Do you feel broken? Do you find yourself hiding in your brokenness, leaning on others, or trying to stand alone? Take a few minutes to write about how you are handling your heartache. Has God allowed you to use your pain to help someone else along the way? If not, I promise He will in time. Ask God to show you ways you can make a difference in the life of a broken friend when you are ready to take that step.

_____

_____

_____

_____

_____

_____

_____

_____

_____

_____

_____

_____

FACING DAWN

When You're Called to Rejoice...and Don't Want To

Rejoice with those who rejoice; mourn with those who
mourn.
Romans 12:15

The day slipped by and the choice had to be made.

Would I make the phone call or simply pretend it hadn't
entered my mind?

I couldn't lie.

It had not only entered my mind,

It wouldn't leave my mind.

Today was the birthday of one of Nick's lifelong best friends.

Nick had never missed his party ever....until now.

I wrestled all day with how to handle the reality that Nick
would never be at Jon's party again. I didn't really want to
know the details of what Nick might be missing, but I did
want Jon to know I loved him and remembered.

After all, he misses Nick too.

So, I finally got the nerve.

I dialed his number and Jon's mom, who is one of my dearest friends, answered the phone. I knew it must be hard for her too.

I said, "I called to wish Jon a "Happy birthday."

So Jon came to the phone and I sang,

Happy birthday to you,
Happy birthday to you,
You don't look like a monkey.....
And you don't smell like one either!

I had to do something to make us both laugh.

Then I said, "I love you, Jon."

And he sweetly replied, "I love you too, Tammy."

Then my voice broke as I said "bye."

Nick's wind chime began to blow behind me as I stood alone in the darkness of our backyard.

I hung up and cried until I could cry no more.

I looked up toward Heaven and there it was. One bright star all alone in the sky, almost exactly like the weekend Nick had died. (A large star and a small one had lit up the sky on the night Nick passed away. We felt sure it was Nick and Adrienne's way of saying "We're together!")

I said out loud, "I love you, Nick, so much. I always will."
And then I told God I loved Him too, but that there was so
much I would never understand while on this earth.

Now I'm back in the house trying not to feel blue.

Cooking supper.

Doing laundry.

The normal things a mom has to do.

But I'm thankful.

Thankful God pushed me to call Jon.

I really do want to rejoice with those who rejoice.

I want to be a big girl.

But, oh, sometimes it's not easy.

REFLECTION TIME:

Being happy for other people isn't as easy as being sad with them, but God calls us to lives where we do both. Are you struggling to be happy for a friend who is happy? If so, write about how you feel. In the process, you may discover that God has a blessing tucked away for you in your honesty.

_____

_____

_____

_____

_____

_____

_____

_____

_____

_____

_____

_____

_____

_____

On a Snowy Day

"Come now, let us reason together,"
says the LORD.
"Though your sins are like scarlet,
they shall be as white as snow."
Isaiah 1:18

I love snow!

Kids love snow!

Teachers really love snow!

When the weatherman even hints that snow is on the way,
you can feel the excitement in the air in our small town.

Yesterday as I was subbing, I heard teacher after teacher talk
about the fact that next week the weatherman is "calling for
snow!"

What is it about snow?

For me, I think it's the thought that the world might shut
down temporarily causing everyone to simply stay home and
cuddle up under blankets and sip hot chocolate.

White roads unmarked by tires or even footprints.

Tree branches drooping with piles of white fluff.

Snow covering up mud puddles and potholes.

The absence of imperfections in my landscaping covered by a blanket of white perfection.

Snow truly "evens out" the world's good and bad into one big sweeping view of white beauty.

In the beauty of a freshly-fallen snow, I believe we feel a sense of peace.

Watching snow fall from the sky tops my list of favorite things to do.

Witnessing the transformation from green and brown scenery to a canopy of whip-cream-glazed rocks, gravel, weeds, broken toys, and bare branches takes my breath away.

Snow offers the chance for old things to become "new."

Isaiah 1:18 tells us,

"Come now, let us reason together,"
says the LORD.
"Though your sins are like scarlet,
they shall be as white as snow."

Maybe our deep longing to be white as snow is what makes us long for things like
snow days,
sledding,
building snowmen,

creating snow angels,
eating snow cream,
sipping hot chocolate,
cuddling under a blanket,
and
catching snowflakes on our tongue.

God never ceases to amaze me with His ability to create opportunities that cause us to long for the whiteness of snow.

As our town prepares for a possible "snowy week" next week, I hope I am preparing with even more excitement for the day when my faith will become sight.

I long for the day when Jesus welcomes me to Heaven and proclaims that I am "whiter than snow!"

I wonder if Nick, Adrienne, Natalie, Tyler, Brittany and so many other precious children who left their families too soon are playing in the snow in Heaven.

Can you even imagine how beautiful the snow will be there?!

Peaceful, beautiful, perfectly white-

With no need for mittens, scarves, hats or coats!

Now that sounds like Heaven to me!

REFLECTION TIME:

Snow days have always been my most favorite days. They were Nick's favorite too. I love to imagine him enjoying his favorite kind of day in Heaven. Write a little bit about what Heaven might look like on your favorite kind of day. How does thinking about this perfect kind of day bring comfort to your hurting heart? Tell God how you feel. He is listening.

_____

_____

_____

_____

_____

_____

_____

_____

_____

_____

_____

_____

_____

_____

When You Feel Useless

Dear friends, do not be surprised at the painful trial you are
suffering, as though something strange were happening to
you.
But rejoice that you participate in the sufferings of Christ, so
that you may be overjoyed when his glory is revealed.
I Peter 4:12

*The righteous cry out, and the LORD hears them; he delivers
them from all their troubles.
The LORD is close to the brokenhearted and saves those who
are crushed in spirit.
A righteous man may have many troubles, but the LORD
delivers him from them all.
Psalm 34:17-18*

Well, the snow has arrived!!

So have piles and piles of wet coats and soggy gloves!

Yesterday as Olivia and Todd were preparing for some
sledding fun, Olivia came to me with a problem.

Her snow pants, which have been part of our snow-day events ever since her oldest brother Erich wore them as a young boy, had a broken strap and even the safety pin holding the strap together had worn out over time.

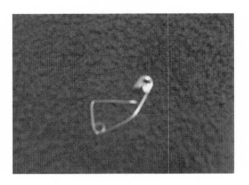

Fortunately, I was able to replace the broken safety pin with a new one and send her on her way to have fun in the snow. I looked at the pin and thought to myself, "Well, you did a good job for Erich, Evan, Todd, and Nick, but your days are over," and I set the pin aside not really thinking another thing about it.

A little later, Cameron (Olivia's friend) came to me with yet another problem. Her snow boot shoelace had a knot that was too tight for her to get out with her little fingers. I worked and worked on the knot and realized it was just too tight for me to wiggle loose with my human hands. Suddenly, I remembered the broken safety pin.

I got it off the shelf and using its sharp point I was able to loosen the knot enough to untie the shoelace totally.

We retied her boot, and she went happily on her way, ready to sled!

I looked down at the pin and had an entirely different thought.

"You still work! You still have a purpose!" It's just different now!"

God spoke to me in that very moment through a simple, broken pin.

Like the pin, I feel so broken. I feel so "set aside" at times.

A mom "set aside" from being Nick's mom.

A caregiver "set aside" from taking care of my sick child.

A teacher "set aside" from teaching, because I just couldn't juggle it all at once.

A friend "set aside" from some of my friend's lives because they seem to feel awkward around me right now.

A church member "set aside" from many of my ministry passions, because I've been so consumed with my family.

The list goes on and on and on.

I bonded with a broken pin today.

I had looked at the pin earlier, sitting on my bathroom shelf.........

bent, stretched beyond its capabilities, unable to hold things together anymore, and I had thought,

"Poor pin. Poor, useless pin. You look like I feel."

You can probably imagine the joy that stirred in my heart when I realized that the very pin I had empathized with just minutes before was the only thing that came to my mind when I couldn't undo the knot in Cameron's boot.

As Cameron left the room, I looked down at the pin and felt such excitement!

The pin was broken, but it still had a purpose!

Oh, thank you, God, for promising to use me in spite of my brokenness. And in fact, you promise to use me in ways only possible because of my brokenness.

Lord, you truly can make all things new!

REFLECTION TIME:

Sometimes when our hearts are broken, it's easy to feel like we have no purpose, no reason for doing "the next thing" on our list of things to do. How can God use your brokenness today to make a difference in the world?

_____

_____

_____

_____

_____

_____

_____

_____

_____

_____

_____

_____

_____

With a Sense of Peace

"I have told you these things, so that in me you may have peace. In this world you will have trouble. But take heart! I have overcome the world."
John 16:33

A car accident took the life of a four-year old on the interstate just a few miles from our home recently. Snowy roads caused the driver to lose control.

A friend of ours is at the hospital this morning after spending the night in the emergency room with his wife. Doctors are not sure what has caused her seizure.

Another friend of mine stopped by yesterday to talk. She's worried about her son's health.

As I read the verse above, I try to find comfort in its words, knowing that Jesus promises peace to each of these families in the midst of their troubles.

As I read it, I'm also reminded of the night I read it to my mom in the hospital years ago when Nick was having terrible trouble with his IV. We had been told by a nurse that she would be back around 4am to give Nick medicine through his IV but she couldn't promise that it would survive the next dose of medicine because his veins were so weak. These words fell on Nick's ears after many, many tears and several new IVs throughout the day.

Nick was exhausted. I was exhausted. My mom was exhausted. Tim had gone home to be with our other kids for the night, and we felt very alone in a hospital room several hours away from home.

As we sat in the semi-dark room that night, I read from a devotional book and stumbled upon John 16:33, reading it aloud to my mom, "*I have told you these things, so that in me you may have peace. In this world you will have trouble. But take heart! I have overcome the world.*"

I still get a little tickled when I think of my mom's response as she lay in the hospital bed next to Nick. She didn't even roll over to talk to me. From the depths of her pillow and her heart, I heard the sad but heartfelt words, "Well, He's not here yet."

I guess that's where the lifelong question of "Where is God when you need Him?" comes from.

We believe God created this world.

We believe He is the Master of the Universe.

And then we get phone calls, emails, knocks at the door.......

All of which deliver news that does not ring with the sound of peace.

So, I sit here this morning looking out at a beautiful snow glistening in the sunshine, and I realize that it's not as much about God promising "earthly peace" as it is about Him offering "inner peace."

After I read that verse to mom in the darkness of Nick's hospital room years ago, I had this spiritual nudge to go call a friend and ask her to pray with me.

A nurse happened to walk by and see me crying as I talked on the phone. She approached me and realized I was struggling, so she sat down in front of me and actually prayed out loud as we sat on the hospital floor. She then came and administered Nick's IV medicine herself later that night.

It was an amazing moment in Nick's journey through cancer.

It was God bringing a little peace to our world that was full of trouble.

For Nick, I don't have to worry anymore about IVs going bad or MRIs holding devastating news.
Peace has arrived in the most perfect sense for Nick. He has been made perfectly whole and new!

Jesus says, "In Me you may have peace."

This means that even in my brokenness and loss I can have a deep abiding sense of God's presence and love.

You can too.

REFLECTION TIME:

Do you ever struggle to feel a sense of peace in your life? God longs for you to know He is with you even on the most difficult days, so what can He do for you today in order to demonstrate His love and help you feel His presence? Ask Him to bring the peace you so desperately long for in a way only He can do. Come back to this devotion in a month or so and write about how God answered your prayer.

_____

_____

_____

_____

_____

_____

_____

_____

_____

_____

_____

_____

When You're Feeling Crushed

A happy heart makes the face cheerful, but heartache
crushes the spirit.
Prov. 15:13

Even though I know deep inside that grief is a journey that
takes time, I still struggle on days when I just can't shake the
sadness.

Today was one of those days.

I worked on some of the plans for the foundation dinner this
weekend.

Todd had choir practice this afternoon, so Olivia and I ran to
Ashland for more picture frames and a few things at
Walmart.

Why is Walmart so hard for me?

I guess it's difficult because I remember how much Nick
loved shopping with me. He was my shopping buddy!

After we shopped, I asked Olivia if she wanted to grab
something quick to eat and we decided to run through
Fazoli's.

As I took a breadstick out of the bag, I had such a flashback of Nick grinning and waiting for a Fazoli's employee to bring more breadsticks to our table. He had so much fun no matter where we were! I miss his joy! I miss his love for living!

When we got back home, I just couldn't let go of my feeling of sadness. It haunted me all day.

I cleaned the bathroom upstairs, dumping out every drawer and pulling out everything under the sink. Maybe purging something would purge me of this blue feeling deep inside my soul.

But still the sadness in my heart consumed me.

Crushing my spirit.

Pressing my chest to the point of physical pain.

I know that Nick is in Heaven. But I also know he's not with me.

Help me regain my eternal perspective, Lord. Help me, please.

I am weak today. Feelings of insecurity dance in my mind.

Give me strength, Lord.

Create in me a new heart. A happy heart.

I know You can. I trust You.

I'm waiting for signs of a cheerful face, and believing it will arrive in His time.

REFLECTION TIME:

Sometimes grief overtakes us in the most unexpected moments, leaving us feeling crushed and defeated. Don't be afraid to write about your feelings of despair. God knows and He cares. Share about a time in your grief that was especially painful. Write a prayer to help you on days when you feel crushed, asking God to bring back a cheerful face in ways only He can. Thank Him for promising to hear and answer your every prayer.

_____

_____

_____

_____

_____

_____

_____

_____

_____

_____

_____

_____

FACING DAWN

When You're Trying to Heal

When they saw the star, they were overjoyed. On coming to the house, they saw the child with his mother Mary, and they bowed down and worshiped him. Then they opened their treasures and presented him with gifts of gold and of incense and of myrrh.
Matthew 2:10-11

While he was in Bethany, reclining at the table in the home of a man known as Simon the Leper, a woman came with an alabaster jar of very expensive perfume, made of pure nard. She broke the jar and poured the perfume on his head.
Mark 14:3

From the moment He entered this world, Jesus' presence stirred a desire for gift giving.

Wise men travelled many, many miles to place their gifts at Jesus' feet. Not every-day kind-of gifts either, like swaddling clothes, blankets, rattles, or bibs.

No, they brought gifts fit for a King. Things like gold. These wise men knew who Jesus was!

Years later, a woman who was shunned by many because of her sinful past, found herself at Jesus' feet pouring out what could have easily cost her life's savings. On Jesus' feet, she emptied her alabaster jar filled with expensive perfume. She, too, knew who Jesus was!

I especially love Mark's account of this story, because he adds the detail of Mary "breaking" the jar at Jesus' feet.

What is it about a broken alabaster jar that makes the story of Mary pouring her perfume on Jesus' feet so beautiful to me?

I connect with broken things. They speak to me like whole things just can't. I'm drawn to the word "broken" in any story.

That's why my Christmas gift from some of my friends and their daughters, who happen to be Olivia's friends, will forever be one of my treasures.

The night they surprised me with my Willow Tree Nativity set, I cried.

I love Nativity sets!

And Mary, the mother of Jesus, had been on my heart in such a huge way ever since Nick died. I kept thinking of how she was called "blessed" and how she was "chosen" to be the mother of Jesus yet would eventually face the agony of watching her son die on a cross. I wondered, "Did she really know how broken her heart would be one day be as she held her baby boy close to her side surrounded by farm animals and straw?"

Mary reminds me that I am blessed to be Nick's mom, even though I had to let him go.

So, when I saw the boxes from my friends and gazed at the pictures of each beautiful piece of the Nativity scene, the "old" me wanted to go home and quickly get it all set up, but we were leaving for Oklahoma the next morning and I had so much to do.

I knew that in my rush I might break something.

So, I placed all the boxes in my closet and couldn't wait to get back from our trip and open every box!

Finally the day arrived!

I sat on the floor and began to unpack each figurine one by one.

As I was taking out one of the wise men, though, his hands along with the "gift" he was holding fell on the floor in front of me.

My first thought was, "I'll just ask the girls if I can exchange this piece," because I was confident it was broken before I even took it from the box.

The longer I sat and looked at him, though, the more I fell in love with this particular wise man.

Hands gone, arms lifted up, wanting to give something to Jesus but unable to give in his broken state................

This wise man looked just like I felt!

So, I decided to fix him myself.

I carefully placed very strong glue on a toothpick and balanced the piece just right in my sock drawer for an entire day so that the broken part could bond with the arms. When I turned him over, you could see a faint line where the break had occurred and remnants of glue around the edges of the break

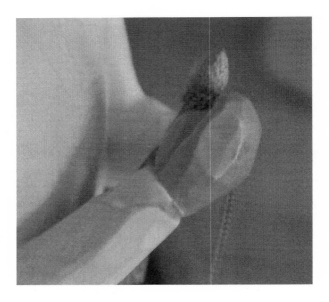

And I thought to myself.......

Wise man, you are me!! You are trying to give something to Jesus, but you are showing signs of brokenness and an effort to heal.

Last night as I was walking up to Olivia's room to take pictures during her little fashion show (she was trying to decide what to wear to Nick's foundation dinner), I stopped and took some pictures of the nativity set and my favorite wise man. I had planned to write about him one day in the future.

The amazing part came when I sat down in Olivia's room to straighten her hair as she was listening to a Point of Grace CD. I was just about to change it to one of my favorite songs when Olivia said, "Oh, let's listen to this one first. It's really good."

As I sat and listened, it was all I could do not to cry.

Imagine how I felt when I heard the words, "Heal the wound, but leave a scar."

I knew God was saying, "It's time to share the story of your broken wise man!"

I immediately knew that my wise man was supposed to be broken when I opened the box.

I instantly realized that God wanted me to keep my figurine with his broken arms.

It was all part of God's plan.

He knows my heart is broken, and I'll always have a scar.

And He made it very clear tonight that I'm going to be okay.

REFLECTION TIME:

I struggle with the phrase, "time heals." I like to say, "time softens." I don't think we ever fully heal from broken hearts. I do believe, though, with God's help the brokenness can be mended enough to become a beautiful scar. Write about some of your scars. What have you learned through your times of brokenness? Do you know that God still longs to use you? If you are struggling to give in your brokenness, ask God to help you. He hears your prayers and cares about you deeply.

_____

_____

_____

_____

_____

_____

_____

_____

_____

_____

_____

_____

When You Don't Know How

Always be joyful. Never stop praying. Be thankful in all circumstances, for this is God's will for you who belong to Christ Jesus.
~ 1 Thessalonians 5:16-18, NLT

When I read this passage, I realize God never meant for us to "wonder" how He felt about us having joy, spending time in prayer, or feeling thankful.

Using words like "always," "never," and "all," He certainly didn't leave room for things like...

"when I feel like it," or

"tomorrow," or

"when I'm ready," or

"when life is going my way."

No, He definitely tells it like it is.

And His will is this...

<u>Always</u> be joyful. <u>Never</u> stop praying. Be thankful in <u>all</u> circumstances.

These are difficult words to swallow when your heart is broken and your life has been turned upside down by the loss of someone you love.
The only way I can read the words in this verse and not feel somewhat guilty for my lack of earthly joy, my struggle to keep praying, and my inability to feel thankful is to think of what Jesus did for me on the cross.

When I take the focus off of myself and place it on Him who died for me, suddenly my heart begins to feel a little lighter.

Jesus conquered death, giving us a living Hope! That is a perfect reason to feel joy! He kept talking to God to the very end. Even after He had been beaten, ridiculed and nailed to tree, He still looked up and talked to His Heavenly Father. Because of what He did on the cross on that Friday long ago, I can surely muster the strength, even in my grief, to say "thank you" today.

Why?

Because without His supreme sacrifice, where would I go with my heartache?

So, today, as I struggle to face dawn, I'm going to lean back and soak in God's will for me………………

Constant Joy. Unending Prayer. Unconditional Thanksgiving

It's actually kind-of freeing to know I don't really have a choice!

REFLECTION TIME:

If you had to place your joy level on a scale of 1 to 10, where would it fall today? How about your prayer life and feeling of thankfulness? Don't feel bad if you give yourself a 1, but take time today to talk to God about why you are struggling and then spend a few minutes thinking about what Jesus did for you at Calvary. I think you'll find your number rising as you intentionally ask God to help you in all three areas.

_____

_____

_____

_____

_____

_____

_____

_____

_____

_____

_____

_____

_____

When There's Nothing Left to Give

Each one should use whatever gift he has received to serve others, faithfully administering God's grace in its various forms. If anyone speaks, he should do it as one speaking the very words of God. If anyone serves, he should do it with the strength God provides, so that in all things God may be praised through Jesus Christ.
I Peter 4:10-11

It probably started as a rebellion.

This tube of toothpaste was going to be used, and used, and used, and used, and...............

you guessed it...........used

.........until I decided to throw it away!

Honestly, it was becoming like the empty roll on our toilet paper holder.......

But that's a story for another day..............

This tube of toothpaste fascinates me.

Every day, I manage to squeeze out just enough to brush my teeth one more time.

Amazingly, so does Tim. I'm wondering who else slips in our bathroom and does the same thing?

No one has complained about this tube's lack of resources. It's as if just enough toothpaste arrives every morning to get us through another day, every single day!

The more I look at this toothpaste tube, the more I appreciate how it symbolizes the way our family is living in our grief.

To be honest, it symbolizes how anyone lives who is trying to survive a difficult season in life.

One "squeeze" at a time. Not feeling "stocked up" on much of anything.

Feeling empty, as if "life" has literally been squeezed right out of you.

Somehow God, in His amazing wisdom, knows the secret to making our empty tube of toothpaste somehow still have worth.

He somehow provides just enough strength for us to do what we need to do for one more day.

Believe me, there are many days when I would much rather pull the covers over my head and sleep my way through life.

I'm so thankful for a Father who tells me He can provide the strength I need for one more day!!!

Eventually, I believe, he will restore my "tube!" As if through a divine run to Wal-Mart, God will place a "new tube" of strength within me....and within Tim.

For now, I have to keep allowing God to squeeze just enough strength from me to keep me going day by day!

If you're feeling like your tube is almost empty, and you are living one squeeze at a time, I want to encourage you.

God longs to give you just what you need for today!

REFLECTION TIME:

Do you ever feel like you are surviving "one squeeze at a time?" I love that God understands us even in our emptiness and promises to provide just what we need when we need it. Take a few minutes to write about how God is giving you strength to make it through each new day. If you find yourself feeling like you just can't make it through another day, remember what God did for you yesterday and ask Him to help you trust Him with today.

_____

_____

_____

_____

_____

_____

_____

_____

_____

_____

_____

_____

_____

FACING DAWN

When It's Cold Outside

For since the creation of the world God's invisible qualities—
his eternal power and divine nature—
have been clearly seen, being understood from what has
been made, so that men are without excuse.
Romans 1:20

Jesus said to her, "I am the resurrection and the life. He who
believes in me will live, even though he dies...."
John 11:25

Cold, harsh winds.

Lifeless branches.

Frozen ground.

Halting life.

Winter symbolizes death so poetically, doesn't it?

The bitter winds of winter are as painful as the empty, hollow
feelings deep in our hearts and minds in times as we trudge
through our grief.

Winter hangs over us like a portrait filled with faces of those
we miss desperately.

Everything seems hopeless when the once-lush ground seems to have been swallowed up by winter's hunger.

As time passes, we learn to accept this phase of life called winter, sometimes even embracing its beauty as we realize it is part of God's natural order of things.

Then something happens.

Something miraculous.

One day we look and SURE ENOUGH! Life is bursting forth where death seemed to have taken hold!

Once colorless landscapes now burst with purples, yellows, blues, and greens.

I just love springtime! It reminds me that death truly has no power over life.

God makes all things new..............flowers, trees,
bushes.........and US!!

If death has no hold on plants, it definitely has no hold on us!

I find these words so comforting when I think of my sweet
Nick. Oh, the emptiness of life without him. Yet I believe
that just as tiny flowers miraculously appear after a long,
hard winter, Christians arise from death to live a new and
beautiful life with God in Heaven.

Olivia and her friend Cameron helped me photograph our
first signs of spring in Grayson this year!!

We were dropping some things off at church for an upcoming
yard sale when we noticed tiny little flowers popping through
the cold, hard ground right near the edge of the sidewalk.

It was so exciting!

As we looked around we noticed other signs of spring
popping up through piles of leaves!

Peeking through....

Promising new life.....

I think the miracle of spring is one of the things God was talking about when He said that His eternal power can be seen in nature....causing men to be "without excuse."

So, if you're doubting whether there is life after death....Take a walk and see what's happening as winter melts away and spring goes on display!

It's God's way of saying........

"I have the final word on death....

and it is LIFE!!!!!!!!!!!!!!!!!!!"

REFLECTION TIME:

Nature's changing seasons remind us that just as winter follows fall, we know spring will follow winter. Grief feels a lot like winter. What can we trust will follow our cold, difficult season of pain? Write about your feelings today by comparing them to winter and then ask God to reveal signs of spring buried deep inside your heart.

_____

_____

_____

_____

_____

_____

_____

_____

_____

_____

_____

_____

_____

When Life Doesn't Make Sense

What is more, I consider everything a loss compared to the surpassing greatness of knowing Christ Jesus my Lord, for whose sake I have lost all things.

Phil. 3:8

I've been reading a little booklet I picked up at the Beth Moore conference this past weekend, and in it she shares the verse above with some thoughts on "knowing Christ."

She shares that the verb "to know" is "nosis" in the Greek and can be translated "the knowledge," but that the deeper meaning of the verb implies "present and fragmentary knowledge!"

She goes on to talk about how Paul is trying to stress the fact that NO MATTER WHAT HAPPENS, NO MATTER WHAT WE MAY LOSE, nothing compares with even the little fragments of what we already know about Jesus Christ. We may have lots of questions that seem unanswerable, lots of mysteries that seem unsolvable, lots of difficult situations that seem unnecessary, but just resting in the little that we do know about Jesus-the snippets of His story-is enough to declare His SURPASSING GREATNESS!

She then looks at I Corinthians 13 and talks about how the verse that says, "Now I know in part; then I shall know fully, even as I am fully known," uses a form of the word "know" that gives us hope because it means "full and complete" knowledge!

Reading this book has reminded me of a few Sundays ago. I was getting a cup of coffee in the hallway before Sunday school, and I could hear Nick's Sunday school teacher around the corner teaching his lesson to all of Nick's friends.

A sad and panicked pain rushed through my heart as I realized Nick wasn't in there and never would be again, but then almost immediately the Lord placed on my heart this very verse,

"Then I shall KNOW even as I am fully KNOWN!!!!"

Nick doesn't need a Sunday school lesson anymore! He is sitting at the feet of Jesus......KNOWING ALL that we now can only long to know.

I loved what I was reading today about the different forms of the word "know," but I didn't plan to write about it until something happened while I was subbing!

Maybe I should have known by the name of the school (The Prichard Yellow Jackets) that this type of memory was inevitable, but it still took me by great surprise!!!

I had lunch duty, so I was sitting at a cafeteria table with about 45 precious third graders. The boy on my left was telling me one story while the boy on my right was trying to tell me an entirely different one.

While I sat there, trying to eat and trying to soak up their words, a group of kids at the other end of the table began to scream loudly! I quickly looked towards that end of the long table and realized that students were swaying from side to side and screaming. Then I saw it....

A wasp was flying over the table, sometimes dipping down into the middle of the table and then sometimes taking a sharp turn and going up into the air. The kids were hysterical.....I thought "surely not......surely this isn't happening to me.....how will I ever get these kids calmed down." Thankfully, the wasp made it to the end of the table where I had gone to try and "swat it" out of the air and a sweet lunch lady managed to "whack it with a towel" and then stomp on it right there in the cafeteria! The kids burst into applause! It was hilarious.

As we lined up and headed back to the room, the kids couldn't stop talking about the memory. I heard so many different versions of the story that I thought it would be neat to have the kids share their memory in writing from their own perspectives. I told the students that when authors write from their personal perspective their reader gets a more powerful impression of their story. I asked the other third grade teacher if she would have her kids do the same thing. Later, as I read all of their versions of this same little moment in time, I was amazed at how pieces of the story all came together and made a much more complete story than I ever could have imagined on my own.

By reading all of the stories, I learned that....

the wasp flew in through an open window

the wasp landed on someone's biscuit

---

that student still ate the biscuit!

some kids were terrified

some thought it was funny

some kids kept on eating because they didn't want to get stung

some kids tried to dodge the wasp and almost fell out of their seats

the lunch lady used a towel for her weapon

and the list goes on and on.......

It wasn't until I sat and read all of these short and funny stories that I had a clear picture of what had really happened in those few short minutes at lunch today.

Suddenly, I knew how the bee arrived, what he did while he was on the scene, and how his journey had ended!!

Suddenly the words I had been reading about "knowing" Jesus in fragments made so much more sense!

I believe that there will come a day when we will stand before the throne and SUDDENLY just as if we are reading a million notes at one time from a million different perspectives we will have the complete and full story of our lives.................

EVERYTHING WILL MAKE SENSE!!!

The "almost" accidents, the unexplainable losses, every tear, every blessing, every disappointment, every pain and every gain.......

SUDDENLY we will understand them all!!!

From my tiny, human, imperfect view, it is easy to look at life and ask lots of questions.

The secret to peace comes when we remember and cling to the truth that one day we will KNOW all things completely!!!

Until that day we're going to have to live with fragments of the knowledge of the surpassing greatness of Jesus Christ, but that should be enough to keep us pressing on!!!

Thank you Father for "bee"ing faithful, "bee"ing creative in the way You speak, "bee"ing my Father, Savior, Lord, Comforter, Protector, Provider, and so much more!

I "bee"lieve that one day my faith will "bee" sight and I will know even as I am known! My knowledge that my "right now" seems so lacking in details, explanations, reasons......so fragmented.....

will one day be full and complete!!

Thank you for this promise!

And thank you for simple things like a kind lunch lady who took the time to swat a "bee" and save me from a nearly out-of-control and hysterical group of third graders!!!!

"Bee"lieving from my fragmented view!

REFLECTION TIME:

If you're anything like me, you long for more details about how your pain and loss will ever make sense. You probably feel as if you are surviving on little fragments of what it means to know Christ and the power of His resurrection. Take a few minutes today to ask God to reveal more of His plan and purpose to you. Ask Him to make Himself known in mighty ways. And then watch out! You may "bee" in for more than you ever imagined!

FACING DAWN

Looking for Hope

*Therefore, we who have fled to him for refuge can have
great confidence as we hold to the hope that lies before us.*
~ Hebrews 6:18b, NLT

I read this verse yesterday and WOW! I keep reading it over
and over and over......

"We who have fled to Him for refuge"....that would be any of
us who have turned to God in our times of fear, grief,
anxiety, loneliness, or betrayal...........

There's nothing like deep pain to send us fleeing somewhere
for safety and protection.

I love that Scripture acknowledges that fleeing is a normal
reaction in times of need.

I love even more that Scripture tells us what to expect when
we choose to run to Him in our moments of greatest need.

Look what His refuge promises,

"great confidence".....

not just a little confidence but GREAT confidence

not the thought that maybe God will be there for us but the
knowledge that HE is!

I don't know about you, but I need some great confidence these days. I need the knowledge that He is here for me in my heartache.

I need something to hold onto in my pain.

So, I love that this verse goes on to say that our great confidence comes as we "hold on to the hope that lies before us."

Not the kind of hope we cling to when we say, "I hope there's no school tomorrow because of snow," or "I hope I get this or that for my birthday."

Not even the kind of hope we refer to when we say things like, "I hope God answers my prayer."

No, the hope mentioned in this verse is a certainty that comes from knowing that God's promises are true.

In our grief, we hold on to a spiritual hope that is so much more than an earthly "hoping for the best."

This same passage in Hebrews goes on to say,

"This hope is a strong and trustworthy anchor for our souls. It leads us through the curtain into God's inner sanctuary. Jesus has already gone in there for us. He has become our eternal High Priest in the order of Melchizedek."

The hope we have in God literally anchors us to Him as we live in a very shaky, uncertain world.

It also leads us directly into His presence.

Nothing separates us from the love of God, not even in our grief.

We attended a Hindu worship service while we were in India, and I was amazed to see a drawn curtain as we entered the temple.

Even the Hindu religion uses a curtain to separate the worshipers from their earthly high priest.

As the ceremony started, the curtain opened so hundreds of people could watch as the Hindu priest performed a ritual of smoke and fire on and around the Hindu god. It was heartbreaking to see so many Indian people clamoring for just a glimpse into this shrine that represented one of thousands of their gods.

This god, made by human hands, offered no hope to a people stricken by extreme poverty. This god extended no arm of mercy, grace, or love.

Jesus, on the other hand, is our Hope.

When He gave His life for us, the curtain was torn from top to bottom. No longer are we separated from the throne of grace, which we are told in yet another passage can be approached with...................

YOU GUESSED IT!!

CONFIDENCE!!!!!!!!!!!!!!!!!!!!

I recalled a couple other verses today that are so packed with power as I thought about "the hope that lies before us!"

Romans 5:1-8

Therefore, since we have been justified through faith, we have peace with God through our Lord Jesus Christ, through whom we have gained access by faith into this grace in which we now stand. And we rejoice in the hope of the glory of God. Not only so, but we also rejoice in our sufferings, because we know that suffering produces perseverance; perseverance, character; and character, hope. And hope does not disappoint us, because God has poured out his love into our hearts by the Holy Spirit, whom he has given us. You see, at just the right time, when we were still powerless, Christ died for the ungodly. Very rarely will anyone die for a righteous man, though for a good man someone might possibly dare to die. But God demonstrates his own love for us in this: While we were still sinners, Christ died for us.

Isaiah 49:23c
*Then you will know that I am the LORD;
those who hope in me will not be disappointed.*

After reading these promises, I have to sit back and think "WOW!" all over again.

For some reason, God has called me to a life of "disappointing circumstances," but I feel He has "appointed" me to share THE HOPE that does not disappoint.

Today, we celebrate Tim's 44th birthday and reflect on the 17th anniversary of the loss of our daughter.

Tomorrow, we enter the month of May and head towards what should have been Nick's 14th birthday on the 22nd.

I'm definitely having to make a choice today to focus on God's Hope which promises not to disappoint.

I am able to write today because of this deep-rooted confidence in "the hope that lies before us!!"

Jesus will return or I will join Him one day.

I believe that on that day I will immediately understand, know, and embrace Jesus Christ................

Now that is what I call a HOPE THAT DOES NOT DISAPPOINT!!!!!!!!!!!!!!!!!!!!!!!

REFLECTION TIME:

Do you feel disappointed in your grief? Have you fled to God for refuge? Run to Him today. Tell Him how you feel. He understands your disappointment, and He longs for you to have the hope that comes from knowing His Son Jesus Christ as your personal Savior. Give Him your heartache and ask Him to replace it with great confidence in the hope that lies before you.

_____

_____

_____

_____

_____

_____

_____

_____

_____

_____

_____

_____

FACING DAWN

When Your Heart is Aching

From the ends of the earth I call to you,
I call as my heart grows faint;
lead me to the rock that is higher than I.

Psalm 61:2

We survived our first family reunion without Nick.

While I love seeing family from all over the country, I entered this once-every-three-year event with great fear of my emotional stability.

I can't pretend that grief didn't ambush me several times over the three-day weekend.

At one point, we were in an ice cream shop previewing all the flavors when I suddenly remembered the joy Nick always had as he picked mint chocolate chip!!! Last year we spent a week at the beach and Nick picked that flavor every single day! He had the biggest grin as he ate every bite!! Oh, I miss his grin.

Watching all the cousins play putt-putt golf or shuffleboard without Nick in their midst proved to be almost more than I could bear.

The last straw was the sight of Todd and my two nephews sitting at a table for four in a restaurant with an empty seat that should have been taken by Nick.

Deep inside I KNOW Nick is great!!!!!!

Yet my heart still aches every single day.

I've been told it will get easier. I guess in some ways it already has.

Maybe that's part of what's wrong with me today.

I NEVER thought I could live without Nick here, and in many ways I hate that I am able to survive without him.

As I type these words, Nick's wind chime is ringing loudly on the back porch as if he's saying,
"Mom, I'm GREAT!!!!!!!!!"

I keep reminding myself that I placed Nick on God's lap over and over again while he was fighting cancer. I took him back a lot, but I always tried to put him right back where I knew he was safest and most loved.

I have to trust that the last time I placed him there, God decided it was best for me to not have him back.

I'm trying to adjust to that truth......still......eight months later.

God has a way of keeping me going, but sometimes it feels good to just stop and pour out a little of what I stuff down over and over again.

Thanks for allowing me to pour out my heart all over you.

REFLECTION TIME:

Do you ever feel so sad that you've just got to pour your heart out somewhere to someone? Take some time to pour your heart out to God.......your questions, your complaints, your sorrow. They are all safe with Him.

_____

_____

_____

_____

_____

_____

_____

_____

_____

_____

_____

_____

_____

_____

FACING DAWN

Knowing You're Not Alone

II Cor. 1:3-5
Praise be to the God and Father of our Lord Jesus Christ, the
Father of compassion and the God of all comfort, who
comforts us in all our troubles, so that we can comfort those
in any trouble with the comfort we ourselves receive from
God. For just as we share abundantly in the sufferings of
Christ, so also our comfort abounds through Christ.

While attending our family reunion the summer after Nick
passed away, I was surprised to hear that one of our relatives
had lost a 12-year old son named Timmy years ago.

After years of reunions where I have seen him smiling,
laughing, and visiting with family, I learned that he too
walked a painful road of grief as a young father.

And he survived.

He shared how Timmy's life still makes a difference in his
life today. He shared his strong belief in Heaven where all of
our tears will be eternally washed away, and we talked about
how Nick and Timmy are now together!

My husband secretly snapped this photo of our conversation, and I ran across it as I was looking through my pictures after we returned home.

I'm glad to have this photo as a reminder that grief is a road walked by many.

I'm learning more and more every day about the fact that you often have to be on the road of grief before others feel safe telling you about their journey down the same road.

My heart goes out to all of you who walk this road with me, beside me, before me, and after me.

You are not alone.

REFLECTION TIME:

Do you ever feel alone in your heartache? Ask God to send someone to you who understands your pain. If you feel ready to help someone else, ask God to send someone to you who needs a friend who will understand their pain. The longer I live the more I realize that everyone has a story that involves some sort of heartache. Never feel alone in your sadness.

_____

_____

_____

_____

_____

_____

_____

_____

_____

_____

_____

_____

_____

When You Can't Hide

Yet this I call to mind and therefore I have hope: Because of the Lord's great love we are not consumed, for His compassions never fail. They are new every morning; Great is Your faithfulness.
Lamentation 3:21-23

This is one of my favorite places at Carter Caves State Park.

One of my friends spent the afternoon with me here today, walking and talking.

The trees around us had literally grown up, around, and through the gigantic rocks under them.

As my friend and I studied this amazing feat of nature, we decided that just like this tree, Christians are called to grow even in rocky times. In these times of difficult growth, we are often required to show much more of ourselves than we'd really like to and in our transparency we become extremely vulnerable to our surroundings.

I have felt like these trees so many times over the past few years. No part of my pain has been hidden as I've continued to write through my pain. Those who read my words know I am hanging on for dear life to whatever foundation I can find beneath my shaky feet.

Grief reveals so much about our personality that we would rather keep hidden.

Anger

Fear

Insecurity

Doubt

So many roots we don't want the world to see.

These trees reminded me today that even when the road is extremely rocky and I have nowhere to hide my emotions, God still provides a way for me to stay rooted in Him. They also remind me to hang on for dear life and continue to live in spite of my pain.

I'm thankful for how God encouraged me today through nature.

I'm especially thankful that God is the Rock upon which I can expose my roots, feel safe, and find stability.

REFLECTION TIME:

Do you ever feel like grief brings all your emotions to the surface? Do you ever want to hide these emotions but find yourself feeling over-exposed? Share about a time when you wanted to hide but couldn't. Ask God to help you accept the fact that sometimes in grief emotions will surface even when we don't want them to..........but that's okay, He understands.

_____

_____

_____

_____

_____

_____

_____

_____

_____

_____

_____

_____

_____

_____

When You Feel Cast Aside

What is more, I consider everything a loss compared to the
surpassing greatness of knowing Christ Jesus my Lord,
for whose sake I have lost all things. I consider them rubbish,
that I may gain Christ.
Phil. 3:8

Olivia's bright orange bucket caught my eye today as it rested
on the edge of the creek bed.

The contrast of the buckets' cheerful color against the
backdrop of gray rocks struck me and made me smile.

I wondered to myself, "Is this how Christians look to God as
we experience dark seasons in our life?"

Trying to stay bright even in tough times.

Trying to stand out in a way that brings positive results.
Just like this bucket, we all have opportunities to bring a
smile even in our pain. We all have a chance to overflow
with His love, and like this bucket, literally "pour" out His
love on those around us.

It's easy to feel "tossed aside" and possibly like a "misfit,"
especially when we are not feeling so bright and cheery on
the inside.

As Christians, though, we have a job to do even in the gray times of life.

We have to allow God to use us.

I'm sure if Olivia's bucket could have talked, it would have asked, "What is my purpose here in the rocks?"

Knowing that it belonged in the creek catching crawdads, I smiled as God used it to speak to me as it patiently waited beside the moving water.

In grief, we often find ourselves unable to function in our normal roles.

Thankfully, God can use us even as we sit waiting in the rocks of life, feeling broken and hopeless.

Help me, Lord, to pour out Your love to others even when I feel tossed aside. Help me be a Living Water-Sharer!

I'm thankful to be a simple plastic bucket with a not-so-simple job.

REFLECTION TIME:

In your grief, do you ever feel like a water bucket that has been cast aside with no purpose? Take a few minutes to write down some of the ways God used you before your heart was broken. Then share some new ways God could use you in your pain to help others who are hurting. Ask God to help you trust Him as He works to bring some sort of good from your suffering.

_____

_____

_____

_____

_____

_____

_____

_____

_____

_____

_____

_____

_____

_____

FACING DAWN

On an Unfamiliar Road

I will lead the blind by ways they have not known, along
unfamiliar paths I will guide them; I will turn the darkness
into light before them and make the rough places smooth.
These are the things I will do; I will not forsake them.
Isaiah 42:16

Our GPS led us to a crossroad. Not sure which way to turn,
we chose to follow the car in front of us with an
Alabama license plate. We couldn't think of any other
reason this Alabama car would be headed down a country
road in Tennessee except to find the same cabin for which we
were searching. So when they chose the road to the left, we
followed.

Sure enough, they were trying to find the same retreat center as us, but we soon discovered that the road we chose was the wrong one, leading only to a locked and chained cattle gate. Tim and I got out of the car and went to theirs to introduce ourselves. This was a strange setting for a first-time introduction. Normally I would have been terrified about walking up to an unfamiliar car on an unfamiliar road in order to meet unfamiliar people. However, there's something powerful about knowing you are on the same unfamiliar road of grief with someone else that brings a sense of safety to a greeting. We hugged, shared our names, and had a little laugh when we found out that their GPS had led them to the same crossroad as ours.

After visiting for a few minutes, we backed up, turned around, and headed for the other road which led us through the woods to the true "Hiding Place."

As soon as we saw the parking lot and the lodge, we realized we had finally discovered the location for a weekend retreat for grieving parents.

As we unpacked our car, we shared more time with our new "friends" and learned of the loss of their daughter this past winter. Over the weekend, we were able to share more of our pain and sadness, and by the time we said good-bye to this once-unfamiliar couple they had become dear friends.

What is it about sharing an unfamiliar road with someone that draws you together?

Grief often feels like a road that leads nowhere.

If our eyes are open, though, we quickly realize that God longs to safely lead us back to His Hiding Place. And God seems to enjoy sending other people to help us…………....people who are on similar types of roads.

It seems that everywhere I turn I find situations I cannot control. Friends are walking unfamiliar roads that appear to have dead-ends.

These roads are often rocky and end with gates that are locked.

I am so thankful for a God who promises to be our eternal GPS if we simply trust Him, knowing that He is leading the way down unfamiliar roads.

REFLECTION TIME:

In your grief, does the road ahead of you seem scary and uncertain? Do you long to know how you're going to make it through another day, another week, another month, another year? Ask God to help you see His hand in your tomorrow. Ask Him to help you recognize when He is smoothing the rough roads ahead.

_____

_____

_____

_____

_____

_____

_____

_____

_____

_____

_____

_____

_____

With Praise on Our Lips and Tears in Our Eyes

Give thanks in all circumstances, for this is God's will for you
in Christ Jesus.
I Thessalonians 5:18

I never dreamed a retreat especially planned for grieving couples would include such a profoundly joyous moment.

Tim and I had just joined hands with eleven other couples around a gigantic dining table to pray before our evening meal when someone mentioned that we should sing first.

Before I could even think of a song that would make sense in our deep sadness, someone suggested, "Praise God from whom all Blessings Flow."

Overwhelmed with just the mention of this song, my heart was not prepared for the sound of so many hurting voices raising their praise to God together.

It was beautiful!

To think that parents who had lost children in so many sad and difficult ways still had a song of praise left to sing.........

even if the song came through tears...............

was just amazing.

As my eyes surveyed the circle of hurting moms and dads, I was overcome by the determined looks on each face.

Suicide, cancer, diabetes, car accidents, and so many other tragic things had taken the lives of our children, and yet we sang praise to Him who gives and takes away.

Holding hands and lifting some sort of praise to the Creator of the Universe, our group looked like a real-life version of the Whos in Whoville gathered to sing on Christmas morning in spite of all that was missing.

Remember how the Grinch's heart literally grew as he heard the music swelling???

I'd love to think the devil is just as shocked and moved when we turn our pain into praise.

I woke up this morning after having a very sweet dream about me, Nick, and Mom at the hospital.

It brought back so many precious memories that I cried all through my shower.

I miss Nick so much that my heart literally aches.

But even in my deepest agony, I want God to know that the devil, the thief who comes to steal, kill, and destroy, has not won.

I cling to Him who promises MORE! Him who promises
ETERNITY!

I will continue to praise Him from whom all blessings
flow…………………..

Even when it hurts!

REFLECTION TIME:

If you were to join a group of grieving families around a table to sing, what do you feel would be an appropriate song? Do you feel like you could sing a song of praise? If so, what would it be? If not, take a few minutes to tell God how you feel. He understands your struggle to praise Him. He wants to hear what's on your heart. He's big enough to handle anything you have to say.

_____

_____

_____

_____

_____

_____

_____

_____

_____

_____

_____

_____

_____

Trying to Feel Blessed in Spite of the Pain

Luke 1:42
"God has blessed you above all women........"(CEB)

When Mary heard Elizabeth say the words, "God has blessed you above all women," I wonder if she felt great joy and honor.

Did Mary grasp what the Lord was asking when He chose her above all other women to be the mother of His Son?

Suddenly, her life became God's life.

Giving up her days as a young, carefree girl and suddenly becoming the mother of God's Son, Mary surely felt the overwhelming responsibility that was wrapped in swaddling clothes and placed in her frail arms.

Fleeing one town for the next in order to keep this sacred child safe, Mary and her husband trusted God even though they surely wondered how in the world God was going to bring good from their far-from-normal life.

We don't know a lot about Jesus' years growing up as a Jewish boy, but we do know that eventually Mary was faced with the nightmare of watching her Son die the most cruel and painful death imaginable while being mocked by crowds of people who just days before had cheered Him into town.

I wonder if all the things Mary treasured in her heart over the years flashed through her mind as she wept at the foot of the cross.

Moments like.................

The shepherds bowing to worship Jesus as He slept in a wooden manger,

The wise men presenting gifts to the royal toddler,

Losing their twelve-year old Jesus in a crowd and then finding Him in the temple,

Witnessing Jesus' first miracle at the wedding in Cana............

I just wonder if these visions danced before her eyes as she watched Jesus dying, and I especially wonder if she recalled Elizabeth's words, *"God has blessed you above all women........"*

There wasn't anything about the crucifixion that could have felt like a blessing to a mother's heart.

And hearing him gasp the words, "Father, why hast thou forsaken me?" must have torn her heart into pieces.

Where was her Son's Father when He needed Him?

Did Mary cry out to God too?

The hope of Heaven must have pulled her through every new morning after Jesus' death and resurrection.

Knowing He had conquered death must have given her the strength to carry on in spite of her pain.

When I think of Mary's anguish mixed with hope and joy, I suddenly feel as if I can make it through my own grief.

She inspires me to keep facing each new dawn with the hope of Heaven set before me.

She reminds me that God's ways are higher, bigger, and better than my ways ever will be.

I'm thankful that God chose to send Jesus to earth through a real, earthly mom.

She reminds me that being blessed doesn't mean life won't be painful, but it does mean God walks every step of the road with me.

That comforts me today.

REFLECTION TIME:

Do you struggle to feel blessed in your grief? If you do, you're not alone. I struggle too. Ask God to help you recall memories of your loved one that you treasure in your heart. Write some of them down, telling God thank you for each of them. Then write about how wonderful it will be to see your loved one again in Heaven! One day our tears will be turned to joy! Oh, what a day that will be!!

_____

_____

_____

_____

_____

_____

_____

_____

_____

_____

_____

_____

_____

_____

Determined Even Though You Know it's Not Going to be Easy

Luke 19:1-4
Jesus entered Jericho and was passing through. A man was there by the name of Zacchaeus; he was a chief tax collector and was wealthy. He wanted to see who Jesus was, but because he was short he could not see over the crowd. So he ran ahead and climbed a sycamore-fig tree to see him, since Jesus was coming that way.

The rock-climbing wall loomed over the ocean water at the front of the cruise ship, so there was no question about how frightening this feat would be to complete successfully.

Shoes were provided which had been designed especially for maneuvering the surface of this steep wall.

Evan chose the middle, most difficult track. The rocks jutted out in a way that made it appear as if you were going to fall backwards with every step you took.

Maria chose the track to the left which offered a different yet challenging climb. I was so proud of her for making it all the way to the top to ring the bell!

As Maria ventured up, she passed Evan gliding back down. Watching his successful climb surely gave Maria an extra boost of determination to make it to the top!

Todd chose the track on the far right, and truthfully, I was shocked that he decided to take on this challenge. He has a HUGE fear of deep water, and I never dreamed he would be willing to climb to a height where he could see the ocean so clearly. But he did, and he made it to the very top!!

After they all made it down, my sister video-taped them as they shared their "secrets" to rock climbing! The way she interviewed them was so cute....as if they had just finished some sort of Olympic event on live TV.

When I look back on these pictures, it's easy for me to see how life is a lot like rock-climbing.

First, we have to face it head on and KNOW that it's not always going to be easy.

Then we have to make sure we're equipped to face the challenges that come along the way.

Just like Evan, Maria, and Todd faced different types of climbs, it's also good to remember that not everyone is going to face the same kinds of struggles. When I remember that truth, I'm less likely to feel some sort of injustice because of the pain I have had to endure as a mom who has lost two young children.

It's also good for me to remember that just as Evan's successful climb encouraged Maria to keep climbing there are people around me who are facing things I have already faced. When they see me "surviving," they are encouraged and realize that they too can make it if they just keep on climbing....in spite of the pain.

Todd didn't let his fear keep him from climbing, and I don't want fear to keep me from moving forward.

I want to be able to ring the bell someday in my "spiritual climb!"

I don't want to stop even when it feels like I'm falling backwards.

I want to help others who may feel like they're slipping....so that they will know THEY CAN DO IT!!!!!!!!!!!!!!!!!

Life is tough.

Looking up is the only way to keep climbing with hope.

LOOK UP as you face dawn and never forget that the tougher the climb the more rewarding the ringing of the bell will be!!!! (As I write these words, I'm praying I can remember them when things get tough.)

I often "fall short" in life (maybe not physically but definitely emotionally and spiritually, but like Zacchaeus, I'm going to climb whatever I have to climb in order to see Jesus!

I know it will be worth it!!!

It'll be worth it for you too!

REFLECTION TIME:

In your grief, do you ever feel like you're trying to make it up a climbing wall while hanging on for dear life? Can you close your eyes and imagine how exciting the day will be when you reach the top, accomplish your goal, and ring the bell – declaring that you have not given up along the way? Compare your journey through grief to something else that is difficult. Ask God to help you press on, looking up to Him for strength and hope all along the way!

Struggling to Understand

Psalm 31:14
But I trust in you, O LORD; I say, "You are my God."

I remember the morning of Olivia's 12th birthday.

She was having a kind-of "blue" birthday beginning.

It was a snow day following many other snow days, so she wouldn't be seeing her friends at school like she had hoped. As far as she knew there were no big plans for her special day.

It was just another regular day in Olivia's mind.

I, on the other hand, was trying to "sneak" around and get everything in order for her surprise party that evening.

I vividly remember feeling a little sorry for Olivia, though, because she had no clue anything special was coming She attempted to invite a few friends over to play in the snow, but they all seemed to be busy. Little did she know they were all planning to surprise her in just a few hours by arriving for her surprise party.

As I left the house to run some errands, Olivia sat alone on the couch watching a cartoon. I leaned back inside the door and said, "Olivia, everything I'm doing today is for your birthday. Trust me. It will be a good day." And then I left.

Eventually a few friends did show up to go sledding, which definitely helped pass the afternoon; but as I was driving from our house to a few stores in town to take care of some birthday errands, I remember clearly the feeling that overcame me as I felt God speaking to my heart,

"Tammy, you are just like Olivia. You do not understand all the things I have waiting for you. The plans I am orchestrating at this very moment so that one day there will be a celebration like you have never seen or could even imagine. Please just trust me."

I felt so reborn in that moment.

It was as if something clicked inside of me that I already believed was true.

Olivia had to make a choice to either trust me and have a great day or not trust me and have a miserable day, and God was calling me to do the same thing with my life of grief.

He was calling me to choose to trust Him even though life did not make sense at the time.

We all have a choice to make every day, too.

We can either trust God and have a great life in spite of our pain or not trust Him and be miserable until our time comes to go Home.

So, when I read about a breakthrough in brain tumor research, I have to take a deep breath and not get angry because the discovery came too late for Nick.
When a friend is struggling because of an unfaithful spouse and I can't fix the problem, I have to pray that God will work in ways I simply cannot.

When another friend is deep in grief and I'm not sure what to say, I have to pray that His Comfort will be enough.

When I watch the news and see the devastation in places like Haiti or Japan,

I have to keep trusting God.

Not that He caused the cancer or the divorce or the loss of another child or the earthquake or tsunami,

but that He will take the imperfections of this world and somehow use them to draw people closer to Him.

I watched a movie tonight with Olivia that I had never seen.

The people in the "perfect world" had no worries, no problems, no need to even walk............they floated through space being fed and entertained constantly. But guess what?

They became bored and started to grumble. Nothing made them happy. Finally, they discovered a way back to planet earth where they again had to grow crops and work and rebuild destroyed cities…and suddenly they were happy!

God knows us better than we know ourselves!

Perfection on this planet is never going to happen. Even if it did, we would never appreciate it for long in our earthly bodies.
So, God uses our pain, sadness, and questions to teach us compassion and trust. He uses our struggles to draw us back to Him over and over again.

Today, our son's girlfriend was in a wreck and totaled her car. Thankfully, she was not injured.

While I am incredibly happy that Maria was not hurt, I am equally sad that my friend's daughter lost her life in a different car accident just a week ago.

In the same way, I'm very thankful that many kids are cured from brain cancer because of new kinds of treatment options, but I am also very sad that Nick's cancer was not curable.

What do I do with these conflicting emotions?

I believe God wants me to do every day exactly what I wanted Olivia to do on her birthday.

Trust.

Simply trust.

When I trust, I am free to stop questioning. I am free to rest in the promise that one day my faith will be sight!

And oh, what a glorious day that will be!!!!

REFLECTION TIME:

Is it difficult for you to trust God in your pain? Don't be afraid to tell Him how you are feeling. He longs to hear your honest prayers. He longs to show you ways that He is working to make all things beautiful in His time. One day we will stand before His throne and all our tears, doubts, and fears will be washed away in the presence of Him who created us and loved us with an everlasting love. Until then, He asks us to do one thing.................trust Him!

_____

_____

_____

_____

_____

_____

_____

_____

_____

_____

_____

_____

Hanging on For the Ride

Nahum 1:7
The LORD is good, a refuge in times of trouble.
He cares for those who trust in him.

I've been watching Joyce Meyer this morning and I feel so inspired, strengthened, and renewed!

She's been talking about the story of John the Baptist from Matthew 11. In this particular story, John the Baptist, who is in prison, hears about all the work Christ is doing in a town nearby. John sends his disciples to Jesus with this question, "Are you the one who was to come, or should we expect someone else?"

See, John the Baptist was surely wondering "Why in the world am I sitting in jail if you are out there? I have been preaching that you are the one who came to save us." I'm just guessing that a prison cell didn't fit the definition of feeling "saved" even in New Testament times.

Jesus had an answer for John the Baptist, though. He sent John's disciples back with these words, "Go back and report to John what you hear and see: The blind receive sight, the lame walk, those who have leprosy are cured, the deaf hear, the dead are raised, and the good news is preached to the poor. Blessed is the man who does not fall away on account of me."

Jesus KNEW that many would stumble because of Him, because in this life things aren't always going to end in "miracles, healings, and a release from struggles."

Jesus knew that John the Baptist would eventually be beheaded because of his faith. There was no earthly miracle for this prophet.

He was called to walk a painful road.

As I listened to Joyce preach on this story from the life of Jesus, I became so RENEWED. I thought to myself, "Tammy, you are a mess. You are so sad one day, so full of questions. The next day you wake up feeling as if you are walking with Moses or Abraham on the greatest journey of faith ever known to man. You make roller coasters look boring."

As I thought about this for a minute, I realized that the road of grief is a lot like a roller coaster ride.

One minute we're up and one minute we're down.

Knowing that an expert designer created every twist and every turn brings a certain level of peace to even the wildest ride. Security is found in the knowledge that at the end of the ride, no matter how frightened we have been or how much we have screamed, we will say, "That was awesome!"

We were created with a longing for the suspense, drama, excitement, and unknowns of adventure park rides just like we were created for a life with same qualities.

John the Baptist was on the kind of roller coaster pictured above. His coaster was headed down a twisting track in which he had no way of predicting the next turn. His trust was totally placed in the hands of the Creator of his track.

Truthfully, so is ours.

We want to stand back and see our life from the perspective of someone who is watching our life "ride" and saying things like, "Oh, I remember when things were great like that huge hill over there," or "Wow, can you believe we survived that upside down time in our life? I thought it would never end," or "I'm glad we didn't know what was behind those trees before we got there, aren't you?"

We also want to see what's coming next. "Is it a valley or a mountaintop-view? Are we going to be holding on for dear life or sitting back and relaxing for a while?"

When I go to an amusement park, I love watching people in line for roller coasters. Some people are watching the ride with great intensity, evaluating every curve, examining the faces of people on the ride when they get off to see if they enjoyed it or not (that's usually me). Others in line are oblivious to the ride and just enjoying the wait, some are consumed with so much fear that they are being encouraged by those around them with words like, "You can do it. It'll be fun!"

Here's the deal:
We are all on a ride called "life."

Our Creator designed each of our tracks. Some days are ups. Some days are downs. But it is the constant awareness that Jesus truly is WHO HE SAYS HE IS that keeps us pressing on toward Heaven.

We must trust Him in every twist and turn.

We must realize that whether our hands are gripping tightly to the rail in front of us or are thrown up in the air in total abandonment, we are OKAY!

I'm thankful for God's Word and how it shares that even the greatest men in the Bible had questions just like we do. Knowing John the Baptist questioned who Jesus came to save comforts me when I have questions too.

John the Baptist lived a life of extreme ups and downs. He baptized the Son of God and then suffered imprisonment and death because of His belief in Who Jesus was. I'm sure he experienced a roller coaster of emotions along the way. I am comforted knowing God cared for John the Baptist and was a refuge to him in times of trouble. He's our refuge too. In the end, if we keep trusting in Him, we'll walk the streets of gold with John the Baptist and so many other amazing men and women of the Bible!!

What a day that will be!

Now, I call that a ride with a great ending!

REFLECTION TIME:

Do you struggle with being "up" one day and then feeling "down" the next day? I often do. Write out your emotions on an "up" day and a "down" day. Compare your words on both days and find comfort in knowing that you are not alone on your up and down journey with grief

_____

_____

_____

_____

_____

_____

_____

_____

_____

_____

_____

_____

_____

When You're Walking in Grief

I Corinthians 7:29-31
I do want to point out friends, that time is of the essence. There is no time to waste, so don't complicate your lives unnecessarily. Keep it simple - in marriage, grief, joy, or whatever. Even in ordinary things-your daily routines of shopping, and so on. Deal as sparingly as possible with the things the world thrusts on you. This world as you see it is on its way out. (MSG)

As I walked through the Goodwill store in Lexington on Saturday (a favorite place for me and my friend to go together), I happened upon a stuffed animal that I'm guessing was some sort of special pillow but looked like a GIGANTIC SLIPPER.

I put it on the floor and jokingly said to Olivia, "Do you think this would fit Erich?" As I looked down, though, and saw my foot next to the incredibly large, fluffy "dog slipper," I said to my friend Pam, "This is the shoe that grief wears."

The more I looked at it the more it spoke to the deepest part of my emotions.

See, grief is so much like this slipper.

Grief is big.

Grief makes walking difficult.

Grief doesn't match the shoe next to it.

Grief causes us to feel different in a crowd - like we just don't fit anymore.

Grief is something that never seems comfortable or "right." At the same time, like this fuzzy, soft, cozy slipper, grief can be a comforting emotion to curl up with on a rainy day when you need to simply face the reality that you "feel sad or blue."

Grief doesn't judge.

Even when we get use to walking with grief, it's always with us. It's as if our foot has gotten use to carrying the over-sized footwear.

I had to buy this huge slipper! I wish I had one to mail to each of my grieving friends.

When I showed it to Tim last night and said, "This is the shoe grief wears," I think he thought I had lost my mind. I smiled and said, "Really, I'm serious. I'm going to wash this, and I may just sleep with it." He smiled and said, "Ok."

I love when God works in ways that seem a little silly to the world. He sent an enormous dog slipper to a Goodwill store in Lexington, Kentucky, for me. I'm thankful God longs to take things as complicated as our grief and make them as simple to understand as an oversized slipper.

I Corinthians 7:29-31 says,
"I do want to point out, friends, that time is of the essence. There is no time to waste, so don't complicate your lives unnecessarily. Keep it simple -in marriage, grief, joy, whatever. Even in ordinary things-your daily routines of shopping, and so on. Deal as sparingly as possible with the things the world thrusts on you. This world as you see it is on its way out."

This passage speaks to me today.

Tammy, keep your grief as simple as this slipper. Wear it, take it off, hold it, even cuddle with it, but don't become entangled in it.

I'm thankful that God led me to this slipper.
Because....................

This is the shoe that grief wears, and I needed to know what it looked like.

It's not as scary as I once thought.

Trusting Him for the strength to continue to walk in a shoe that often seems too big for me to handle...Thankful that I now know I can take it off and feel safe carrying it sometimes too.

REFLECTION TIME:

My grief looks like this big slipper. What does your grief look like? Take a few minutes to write about what your grief looks and feels like to you. Maybe the slipper also works for you. Maybe it's something entirely different for you. Once you've identified what grief looks like to you, write about it..

Grief is your lifelong companion. Give it a name and embrace it. In the embrace, you will find comfort you never dreamed possible.

_____

_____

_____

_____

_____

_____

_____

_____

_____

_____

_____

FACING DAWN

Knowing Life Must Go On

Philippians 3:14-15
I press on toward the goal to win the prize for which God has called me heavenward in Christ Jesus.
All of us who are mature should take such a view of things. And if on some point you think differently, that too God will make clear to you.

One thing I remember vividly about that first year after Adrienne died was how difficult it was to watch life go on for everyone around me in routine, every-day ways.
I remember standing in a friend's bedroom as she put clean sheets on her bed and thinking, "How can her life be so normal?" The last thing on my mind was clean sheets.

It struck me recently, as I was talking with a couple of friends whose daughters play sports with Olivia, that this past year since losing Nick has been very different from the first year after losing Adrienne. Instead of watching everyone else's life return to something normal, I turned to Nick's foundation as my way of "carrying on" and doing something productive yet not as "normal" as washing sheets.

In my conversation with my friends, though, we began talking about last year's softball season, and I realized that I barely remembered anything about Olivia playing softball. I could remember sitting there and watching Olivia at bat one time. Other than that, I couldn't remember much. I realized that for a whole year, I was going through the motions for my family's sake.

This morning, as the sun was shining brightly on the hill behind our house, I was reminded somewhat painfully that this is my eighteenth spring without Adrienne and my second without Nick, and I have to look up to God for comfort and strength so that I can carry on the every-day routines for my family.

Why?

Because life does go on, and I don't want to miss whatever part of life is left for me and my family here.

Without Him and without Hope, I don't think I could make that statement. So today, I'd love to say this to my sweet Adrienne and my precious Nick:

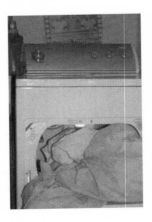

The washer's calling, "Bring the sheets."

The sunshine's beaming, "I'll give heat."

The bedroom's shouting, "Keep me clean."

But I'm stalling, Is this a dream?
Do I really give a care
for sheets and beds that at me glare?

No, I don't, if I may speak...
The truth that from my heart must leak.

But deep within I hear God say,
"Take care of what you have today."

So, routine things I'll strive to do-
Until again I live with you.........

Where "normal" is a **long**-gone word
And doing laundry seems absurd!

I love you both so very much.
I long to feel your gentle touch.

Worship God with all your heart
And while I'm here I'll do my part
To help others find the way
To where you are on this spring day.

REFLECTION TIME:

Has grief made it difficult for you to care about the normal, everyday routines of life? If so, you are not alone. Take a minute to write a poem about how you feel when you attempt to step back into everyday life.

_____

_____

_____

_____

_____

_____

_____

_____

_____

_____

_____

_____

_____

FACING DAWN

With Tears

"..........weeping may endure for a night, but joy
comes in the morning"
Psalm 30:5

We started a new book in my high school reading class
yesterday. A book in which there is mystery, humor, and
loss. Pre-reading discussion always helps kids get excited
about a book, so I started in my normal way.

We discussed the author, the book cover, the title......
We made predictions.......
And then I asked a few questions to help them feel connected
to the main character.

"Have you ever been on a long road trip in a car?" I asked.
Hands shot up all through the room. Oh, the stories I heard
about kids traveling as far as Florida or as close as
Huntington! These kids crack me up.

I shared my memories of riding in the back seat of our
family's car back and forth to Oklahoma as a little girl and
how my sister and I were always sure the other person had
more room...we would draw an imaginary line to make sure
our boundary was not crossed by even a toe!

Then I asked, "Have you ever had a friend or relative move
far away or pass away leaving you feeling very sad?"

Faces changed, but hands went up in the air again.

"My papaw, my uncle, my aunt, my mom".......and the list went on and on........so I shared too.

I shared briefly, but I shared enough to let them know that I was a grieving mom. Most of them didn't know. I told them that there might be times when I wouldn't be able to read. I told them there might be times when they wouldn't want to read. I want them to feel safe in my room with their sadness.

Safe with their tears and safe with not wanting to have tears.

I know my kids on a different level now. We've laughed deeply and we've shared sad memories deeply. Opening my heart was risky, but I am glad I did. It would have been hard to read with the students about sad things knowing that they did not know I was still sad deep in my heart.

If you have sadness in your life, please open your heart to someone. It is freeing just to say, "I am still sad."

So I'll just say it, "I am still sad."

. . . weeping may endure for a night, but joy cometh in the morning." Psalm 30:5

Trying to live with joy even as the tears fall this morning,

REFLECTION TIME:

Sometimes it's difficult to find people with whom we can openly share our sadness without feeling judged. If you have someone in your life you can safely talk to about your heartache, take a minute to thank God for this person. If you don't have a person like this, ask God to send someone into your life who can be your "sadness-sharing" friend. Let's face it. Grief is difficult enough to endure with a friend. No one should have to endure it alone. The good news is this, even when we feel alone, God is still there. Thank Him for that promise today too.

_____

_____

_____

_____

_____

_____

_____

_____

_____

_____

_____

Feeling Captive

"Now I want you to know, brothers and sisters, that what has happened to me has actually served to advance the gospel."
Phil. 1:12

When we hear of someone being sentenced to prison because of their faith in Christ, we do not usually respond with the words, "Praise God!"

There is a natural instinct inside of us that cries out at the injustice.

I am sure the people in Philippi were not happy to hear that Paul was in prison. I am sure that they were praying for his release.

But listen to what Paul had to say about his situation in Phil 1:12, *"Now I want you to know, brothers and sisters, that what has happened to me has actually served to advance the gospel."*

Paul looked through his prison bars and saw those on the outside not as enemies but as men needing the Hope of Jesus Christ.

Paul looked at his tiny prison cell and didn't see confinement and hopelessness. He saw a new opportunity to evangelize.

So many times, I feel bondage in my life either from my grief or from the stress of teaching full-time. Thoughts of hopelessness and confinement easily overtake my mind and soul.

I don't always handle my heartache well.

I don't always handle working full-time well.

In my simple human mind, I convince myself that if I had never experienced loss and if I didn't have a full-time career then I could be such a better Christian witness. I would be happier. I would be freer. I would have more time to write, to be a better friend, to love more deeply.

But you know what?

I really don't think that's true.

Deep inside I know, even though it hurts to type this truth, that "what has happened to me has actually served to advance the gospel."

Losing Nick and Adrienne has catapulted me into a deeper faith. The pain of loss has inspired me to be a more passionate Christian, unafraid to put all my Hope in Heaven and share it with the world!

Being a teacher has provided me with an audience of starving children who want more than a lesson plan filled with the appropriate Common Core Standards and effective teaching strategies.

Today, as I celebrate the freedom of America, I want to look deep inside and proclaim the freedom I have in Christ in spite of the "prison bars" I sometimes feel in this world.

The devil longs for us to focus on the black metal beams looming around us from our past failures, mistakes, or tragedies or from our present life situations.

Jesus, on the other hand, longs to allow His light to shine in between those beams and make a way for us.
A way out of our bondage if we will just allow Him to work!

II Cor. 10:5 is a verse I memorized and say to myself over and over again as I struggle with negative thinking,

"We demolish arguments and every pretension that sets itself up against the knowledge of God, and we take captive every thought to make it obedient to Christ."

If you find yourself feeling as if the situation you are in today is one of hopelessness or captivity, I am praying that, like Paul in the book of Philippians, you can look past the metal bars and see the light of Jesus shining through. In that light you will find peace, Hope, and ways to share His love with others!

REFLECTION TIME:

Is your grief holding you captive? Do you long to feel the light shining through all of your pain, providing some sense of hope in the midst of your pain? Do you long to find a purpose in your suffering? Think about Paul's words in Philippians 1:12. Ask God how He can use your life and your pain to advance the story of His Son and the Hope of Heaven to a hurting world. Be prepared for an answer that requires action.

_____

_____

_____

_____

_____

_____

_____

_____

_____

_____

_____

_____

_____

Asking, "Why?" All Over Again

When the righteous cry for help, the Lord hears and delivers them out of all their troubles. The Lord is near to the brokenhearted and saves the crushed in spirit. Many are the afflictions of the righteous, but the Lord delivers him out of them all. He keeps all his bones; not one of them is broken.
Psalm 34:17-20

I decided to spend a little time tonight trying to go through the inbox of my Yahoo account and do a little housekeeping.

I never dreamed that this mundane task would turn into a walk backwards in time as I discovered email after email related to Nick and his death.

With nearly 5,000 emails in my inbox, I spent several hours sifting through memories trying to decide what to save and what to delete. After narrowing down my inbox to 3400 emails, I decided to stop for the night.

Eyes crossed and fingers weary, I found myself heartbroken all over again.

I try so hard to stay positive and press on every day in spite of my deep sadness, but tonight after rereading some precious words people wrote to me not long after the loss of Nick, I find myself asking the same question I have asked time and time again,

"Why did he have to die?"

Sadly, I know there's no answer. I know I will never understand his death this side of Heaven.

But sometimes it feels good to just type the words, "WHY?"

It feels good to shout my feelings of injustice even though I know there are millions of others who shout the same words every day.

It is liberating every once in a while to just say out loud, "I am sad, and I am not okay with Nick's death."

Yes, I know he is in Heaven.

Yes, I know he wouldn't come back even if he had the chance.

Yes, I know that God can bring good out of the worst situations.

Yes, I know that God still loves me.

But, for tonight, I'm taking a little time to just feel the pain of my loss and remember that it's okay to be sad.

REFLECTION TIME:

Do you ever look back through old photographs or home videos and find yourself grieving deeply all over again? These moments can be so painful and yet so healing as we face our grief head on. Every time we walk close to our loss, I believe God gives us a little more strength for the next part of our journey. Think about some of your most precious memories with your loved one you are missing, and take a minute to reflect on these memories by writing about them. What were you doing that made the memory so special? Can you remember any conversations from that day? Thank God for these precious snapshots hidden deep within your heart and allow yourself time to simply be sad again. God understands your pain and He cares for you.

_____

_____

_____

_____

_____

_____

_____

_____

_____

_____

_____

Ready to be Surprised

He who sows in tears will reap songs of joy.
Psalm 126:5

I was walking through my garden yesterday when I realized that my cucumber plant was actually producing a cucumber!

I don't know why I was so shocked and happy, but I was!

I looked around and discovered that yet another plant was showing signs of this same green vegetable!

Now I have more confidence to watch and wait for tomatoes to appear on my tomato vines!

The Bible says a lot about sowing and reaping, but today I can't help but think of the verse that says, "He who sows in tears will reap songs of joy."

This verse doesn't give a timeline for reaping. It gives no secret amount of days, weeks, months, or even years. It simply says "sow in tears and you will reap songs of joy."

If you find yourself sowing in tears, take heart!

God promises that you **will** reap songs of joy! He doesn't say you "might reap songs of joy" or "hopefully you will reap songs of joy." He says you **WILL** reap songs of joy!

Let your faith in this promise keep you smiling today as you sow in tears.

In time, you will find yourself having a happy day-maybe even a day full of laughter-

When you do, consider it a surprise-cucumber-kind-of day! The harvest is nearer than you think!

I'm longing for the spiritual harvest, aren't you??

REFLECTION TIME:

Grief results in many tears. Sometimes I have cried until I think I can never cry again only to find myself crying the whole next day. Sometimes, though, I realize that I am beginning to feel a bit of joy as I look forward to Heaven and realize that God is using Nick's life to continue making a difference in the lives of so many others. On those days, I begin to understand the part of the verse that says, "we will reap songs of joy." Write about a time when you could sense joy even in the midst of great sadness. How is God using your pain to produce a spiritual harvest? If you're not sure, ask God to show you. I promise your loved one has left a legacy. Allow God to use you to keep that legacy alive and thank God for the times when He allows you to reap a harvest of joy from your tears.

_____

_____

_____

_____

_____

_____

_____

_____

_____

FACING DAWN

Needing a Little Reminder

I arrived at school a little later than I would have liked this morning, thankful for my first period planning time so I could get my dry erase boards ready and papers copied.

Not long after arriving, though, the secretary peeked in my room and asked if I could possibly cover for the teacher next door for the first hour because he was stuck in a traffic jam on the interstate.

Of course I said, "Yes," but deep inside I was having that sick feeling of "I needed this time to get ready for today. What am I going to do now?"

As I sat down at Mr. H's desk and the students began to file in, I looked at his desk and then I knew.........

I knew why he was running late.

I knew why I was sitting there today at 8 a.m. at a desk I had never sat behind much less been near.

I needed to see his desk up close and personal. I needed to read the teacher's prayer that was on a cross sitting on the desk right in front of me.

I needed to read another small plaque that said,

You may not know all the details of your journey or clearly see where the trail is leading, but God will always give you enough light to take the next step."
Roy Lessin

I needed to read more words that were right in front of me,

To know Him is to love Him and to love Him is to trust Him.
Richard Exley

I could have cried as I sat and soaked up all of these messages. My breath almost left me as I leaned back and realized that God, the orchestrator of life, had divinely pulled me into a classroom so close to my own to read words that would draw me nearer to Him.

Tonight, as I reflect on the memories of the day with Olivia curled up next to me in bed, my nose is stuffy and my eyes are heavy but my heart feels just a little lighter.

I walked tonight.
Walking always clears my head a bit, and I was able to stop and visit with a couple friends along the way.

So thankful for friends who understand my unexpected tears as they visit with me - tears which seem to be slipping from my eyes much more easily and much more often lately.

Oh, I love God so much.

I know He hears my prayers, and I know He loves me.
He keeps me looking up even when I am feeling down.

He loves you too!

REFLECTION TIME:

Have you ever felt that God divinely led your steps so that you would encounter something that would draw you nearer to Him? Maybe a rainbow just when you needed it or a beautiful sunrise that especially caught your attention? If you have, write about one of those moments and how it made you feel. If you haven't had this kind of experience, ask God to lead you today to a moment that draws you closer to Him and His messages just for you.

_____

_____

_____

_____

_____

_____

_____

_____

_____

_____

_____

_____

FACING DAWN

When You Slip With Every Step

When I said, "My foot is slipping,"
your unfailing love, LORD, supported me.
When anxiety was great within me,
your consolation brought me joy.

Psalm 94:18

It's another rainy morning here in Kentucky.

As I walked into school, my wet shoes squeaked as I moved across the tile floor.

I almost felt myself slipping with every step I took.

Sometimes, when our feet our slipping on the floor beneath us, everyone around us knows.

They can hear the sound of every step we make.

They can see the look of concentration in our eyes as we try to walk without falling.

I know some of you have squeaky shoes right now, not literally but figuratively.

Your feet are slipping.

You feel unsteady.

I know because we're friends or family.
I know because I love you, and I can hear your unsteady words as we talk.

I can see the ache in your eyes.

Some of you are slipping, and you feel all alone in your pain. Do you feel unsteady as you read these words?

If so, the following words are for you:

God is with you on the wet sidewalks of life.

He's with you on the slippery roads.

His unfailing love will keep you from falling.

Just lean back in His arms and let Him hold you.

Rest in His love today.

There is no greater love than this: God gave up His Son for you.............

Stand firm today....even if your shoes are squeaking.

REFLECTION TIME:

In my grief since losing Nick, I have experienced many days filled with unsteady steps. I wish I could sit with you, look you straight in the eye, and tell you how important it is to turn to God when your feet are slipping. He longs to support you, carry you, be there for you, and love you through your heartache. Are you struggling to walk with steady steps in your grief? Take some time to share with God exactly what you need in order to walk in confidence today. He's listening.

_____

_____

_____

_____

_____

_____

_____

_____

_____

_____

_____

Needing a Happy Ending

James 5:13-16
Is anyone among you in trouble? Let them pray. Is anyone happy? Let them sing songs of praise. Is anyone among you sick? Let them call the elders of the church to pray over them and anoint them with oil in the name of the Lord. And the prayer offered in faith will make the sick person well; the Lord will raise them up. If they have sinned, they will be forgiven. Therefore confess your sins to each other and pray for each other so that you may be healed. The prayer of a righteous person is powerful and effective.

What is it about this passage that torments me?

Shouldn't it be comforting to know that God wants us to come to Him when we are in trouble or sick?

Shouldn't the thought of the elders of the church coming together to anoint someone with oil and cover them in prayer be a beautiful picture in my mind?

Deep inside I know why it torments me so.

I want to pretend I'm okay, and that reading this passage still brings comfort but honestly it doesn't, because Nick was anointed with oil by our elders on three different occasions during his fight with cancer. We believed in the power of these words in James, and we clung to them over and over again.

Yet God chose to take Nick Home instead of giving us the healing for which we pleaded and begged.

I would be lying if I said, "I fully understand God's plan or these verses from James."

I would be lying if I said, "When I read these verses, I feel comforted."

However, I've come A LONG WAY in my grief journey over the past three years, and I do believe this:

Nick is healed!!!!!!

Nick is perfect now!!!!!!

Nick wouldn't come back to this stress-filled, evil world even if I begged him...and I wouldn't want him to leave Heaven now that he is safely there.

And the more I read the passage above, I realize that the portion of the passage above that REALLY MATTERS is where it says that the person who is sick and is anointed with oil will have their sins forgiven!

I love that after James talks about the elders coming to pray, he says, "Therefore confess your sins to each other and pray for each other so that you may be healed."

In God's eyes, healing is a spiritual thing not a physical thing. He wants our hearts purified. He knows that eventually each of us will come to the end of our physical life. It's the condition of our soul that determines eternity!

So, as I sat and read James this morning, I was reminded that even in the Bible prayers weren't always answered with a "yes."

Two examples of unanswered prayer bring me comfort today.

Jesus prayed that He would be spared from the cross, but He wasn't.

Paul prayed that the thorn in his flesh be removed, but it wasn't.

I believe God could have answered both of their prayers in the ways they desired, but He needed them to walk difficult roads for His sake.

Sometimes in life God needs us to walk difficult roads for His sake, too.

If you feel as if you are walking on a difficult road as you face dawn today, please know you are not alone.

God is writing a powerful story with your life journey, and He will use your journey to help others who walk behind you.

Great authors write stories with great endings, and the Bible says that God is the author and perfecter of our faith.

So, I trust and believe that my story and yours will have happy endings.

We get a sneak peek at our happy ending in the book of Revelation.

Soak in these happy-ending promises from the end of God's beautiful story written throughout the Bible.

They make the verses in James 5 a lot easier to read!!!

Revelation 21:4
"He will wipe every tear from their eyes. There will be no more death or mourning or crying or pain, for the old order of things has passed away."

REFLECTION TIME:

Do you struggle with unanswered prayer? Do you question God's plans for your life? Do you feel like you are living a story that can't possibly have a happy ending? Tell God how you feel. He is the Author of your life, and He longs to hear what you have to say. Talk to Him and then claim Revelation 21:4. Ask God to help you remember this verse when you are having extra-tough days. He longs to wipe every tear from your eyes which means it is okay for Him to see you cry.

_____

_____

_____

_____

_____

_____

_____

_____

_____

_____

_____

FACING DAWN

Thinking Up While You're Looking Down

Psalm 42:5-6
Why, my soul, are you downcast?
Why so disturbed within me?
Put your hope in God, for I will yet praise him,
my Savior and my God.
My soul is downcast within me; therefore I will
remember you from the land of the Jordan,
the heights of Hermon—from Mount Mizar.

Psalm 3:3
But you, LORD, are a shield around me, my glory, the One
who lifts my head high.

I was walking through our kitchen the other day, and noticed the sun shining through our curtains in a way I had never seen before. I tried to figure out how this happened, and it never really made total sense to me. I guess the folds in the curtains were just right, but still the fact that no other window was affected by the light must have meant that the clouds were aligned just right over the sun so that only this section of our windows was catching its rays. This is what I saw on our kitchen floor:

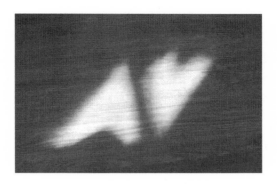

Some might call me crazy for noticing and even thinking that God might be sending a little love from Nick and Adrienne, but it doesn't change the fact that I felt their love in a special way in this moment.

This tiny gift from the sky was enough for me as December 2011 ended and we braced for yet another year of walking in our grief.

I share these pictures as a reminder that in life we will have to face many things that cause us to have a downward look (illness, rejection, loss, pain, sadness, hurt, etc.), but even in times of looking down God can grab our attention and speak from above.

He is omnipresent which means He is in your upward worship just as much as He is in your downcast spirit. He is behind you, before you, beside you, above you, and YES, He is below you............
Trust Him in the good times and lean on Him in the bad times.

REFLECTION TIME:

Do you feel like it is difficult to look up these days?
Remember, God can speak to you from any angle. Ask Him
to speak to you today even if the only place you are able to
look is down. He longs to be the lifter of your head. Ask
Him to help you look up for comfort and strength today. Ask
Him to be the "lifter of your head" today.

_____

_____

_____

_____

_____

_____

_____

_____

_____

_____

_____

_____

_____

FACING DAWN

Filled With Hard Questions

Psalm 86:7
In the day of my trouble I call upon you,
for you answer me. (ESV)

It was late.

I had been on the phone with my friend Martha for over half
an hour - talking, laughing,
listening to her sometimes talk through tears as she lay in a
hospital bed wondering what her tomorrow would hold as
she courageously fought cancer.

My regular workweek bedtime had come and gone, but
sometimes friendship comes before sleep.

It was one of those nights.

Olivia was on the couch next to me as I was finishing my
conversation with Martha. She, too, was full of late-night
questions.

Her classmate Amber who was very ill had experienced a very bad day too and the possibility of air-lifting her to another hospital was the last we had heard about her worsening condition.

Oh, Olivia, our 14 year old philosopher.
She could sit on the steps of any church with a group of elders and ask questions all day long.

I said "bye" to Martha and turned to Olivia who began her inquisition,

"Why does God let bad things happen to good people?

Why doesn't God just stop the devil now if He knows He's going to win in the end anyway?

I know God uses pain to help others, but what about the people who are hurting? How does it help them?

How do I love God? I know He's real, but how do I really love Him?

If something happens to Amber, what will her mom do?

If I were Amber's mom, I wouldn't want anyone trying to tell me about God.

I mean, I believe in God, but sometimes I don't know how to love Him."

The questions continued long enough for Tim to join us, and the moments of silence throughout our conversation hung in the air like the sound of laundry hanging on the line on a windless day.

Stagnant, unmoving, we sat in the quiet room, hoping someone would chime in with a list of perfect answers to our ever-growing list of imperfect questions.

As I glanced at Tim from time to time, I knew deep inside that we both had some of these same questions.

I can't imagine muddling my way through life without God, without the Hope of Heaven, without His love.

But from an earthly perspective so much of our pain seems so unnecessary, doesn't it?

We tried to explain things to Olivia, but the sound of our answers was even bothering me.

Trite answers.

Too simple.

And then, with a trembling lip, Olivia said what I think was on her heart from the very beginning,

And Nick.

I don't remember him anymore.

Why didn't I rub his feet more?

Why didn't I do more nice things for him?

The last thing I remember is leaving for Maddie's house and you saying, "Give Nick a kiss goodbye.," and I didn't because he looked so bad.

That's a hard thing to have as your last memory.

I know what we've been through has helped other people, but how is it helping us?"

Olivia began to cry, and it was all I could do not to join her.

Tim's head went down; and I knew he, too, was sharing in her pain at a level so deep that replying wasn't possible.

I realized last night that grief isn't just a visitor at our house. Grief has moved in to stay.

There will always be nights when one of us becomes especially aware of grief's presence.
Maybe by acknowledging our sadness we can learn to be okay with grief's unexpected visits.

We went to bed with heavy hearts, unanswered questions, and a sense of loss that if often overshadowed by the normal busyness of our lives these days.

I woke up with a headache, eyes aching, and a body moving much more slowly than the hands on our clock.

I keep hearing the lyrics to the song, "I want to know You, I want to seek Your face, I want to know You More," in my head.

Olivia is living out the words to this song, but she's struggling with tough questions these days.

Maybe you have tough questions too.

I wish I had great answers.

I only have Him........

and for today He is enough.

I hope He's enough for you too.

REFLECTION TIME:

Do you find yourself asking tough questions no one can seem to answer? What are some of your questions? Write them down. Ask God to either help you find answers to these tough questions or bring peace when the answers can't be found this side of Heaven. Ask Him to help you face the unanswerable questions with a faith in Him that surpasses all doubts. Believe today that in one way or another God will answer you.

_____

_____

_____

_____

_____

_____

_____

_____

_____

_____

_____

_____

When You Want to Move Forward But You Don't Know How

Exodus 14:14
The LORD will fight for you; you need only to be still.

I love Exodus 14:14.
Recently, I attended an event where the speaker was introduced as someone who considered this verse her favorite one in the Bible.

I smiled and thought, "I love this verse, too!"

Then yesterday, I was reading in Exodus during my regular Bible-reading time and almost laughed out loud when I read the next verse in this same chapter.
For a long time, I had been clinging to the thought of simply "being still" and allowing God to "fight for me" without reading on in this same story.
The Israelites were being pursued by the Egyptians and had reached the Red Sea.
They saw no way out of their predicament.
Raging water on one side.

Enemies on the other.
They began crying out to God and to Moses, and Moses was trying to comfort them.
It was as if Moses was saying,
'"Relax, God has everything under control. Trust Him."
However, as soon as he makes this great proclamation, listen to what God says to him in the very next verse.

Then the LORD said to Moses, "Why are you crying out to me? Tell the Israelites to move on.
Raise your staff and stretch out your hand over the sea to divide the water so that the Israelites can go through the sea on dry ground.(Ex. 14:15)

Sometimes, I think it's easy to give people advice like Moses gave the Israelites.
"Be still. Trust God. He'll fight for you."
I've done it many times.
On one hand, this is very true. God doesn't want us rushing around, fretting, feeling as if we are alone in our battles.
He longs for us to lean on Him, trusting Him with our future.
On the other hand, though, God does expect us to take some action of our own at times.
If you are in a tough spot, cry out to God.
Be still and listen.
THEN.............................DO SOMETHING!
Make some decisions.
Make some changes.
Stretch out your staff and move forward.
Advancing with God takes courage.
Today, I look at Exodus 14:14 and I am strengthened. God is fighting for me.
At the same time, I look at Exodus 14:15, and I am reminded that at some point, I have to take steps forward in my grief and in my faith.
What steps do you need to make today?

REFLECTION TIME:

Do you ever feel as if you don't know what to do next in your grief? Do you feel trapped on all sides by memories, decisions, and sadness? Cry out to God. Tell Him just how you feel. Then be still and listen. But be ready to step forward too. Grief is a journey. Journeys require movement. Don't get stuck in your grief. Allow God to move you forward even if it seems as scary as crossing the Red Sea.

_____

_____

_____

_____

_____

_____

_____

_____

_____

_____

_____

_____

When You Can't Sleep

Numbers 7:1-9

When Moses finished setting up the tabernacle, he anointed and consecrated it and all its furnishings. He also anointed and consecrated the altar and all its utensils. Then the leaders of Israel, the heads of families who were the tribal leaders in charge of those who were counted, made offerings. They brought as their gifts before the LORD six covered carts and twelve oxen—an ox from each leader and a cart from every two. These they presented before the tabernacle.The LORD said to Moses, "Accept these from them, that they may be used in the work at the tent of meeting. Give them to the Levites as each man's work requires."So Moses took the carts and oxen and gave them to the Levites. He gave two carts and four oxen to the Gershonites, as their work required, and he gave four carts and eight oxen to the Merarites, as their work required. They were all under the direction of Ithamar son of Aaron, the priest. But Moses did not give any to the Kohathites, because they were to carry on their shoulders the holy things, for which they were responsible.

Olivia went to bed with a horrible sore throat which meant my next day would hold not only the responsibilities of juggling work and attending a mandatory after-school teacher's meeting but also finding time to take Olivia to the doctor.

Anxiety overcame me in the wee hours of the morning as I tried to process how I would fit everything into my day's schedule.

I decided to get up early instead of tossing and turning.

As I slipped downstairs at 4:30 a.m. to make coffee and read for a bit, I was reminded of what I had read in the Bible just yesterday.

Simply thinking about it, made me smile.

Yesterday morning as I was driving up the hill to the high school where I teach, I was having one of those,
"I really needed a snow day; my schedule is overwhelming this trimester; I don't know if I can do this,"
kind-of beginnings to my day.

On KLOVE they were playing a song that really caught my attention, so I was listening with a little more interest in the lyrics. The chorus kept repeating, "glory, and honor, and power to Him Who sits on the throne." As I tapped my steering wheel and did a little "out loud" power talking to God, claiming His power and asking Him to reveal His glory, I felt as if the Holy Spirit placed the verse in my head that says, "we are more than conquerors." I kept listening to the song and thinking, "Yes, my Father sits on the throne; and glory, and honor, and power are His.......because of this truth, I am more than a conqueror.....I can do this today." My whole mindset changed. I had such a moment of personal revival that I found myself OVERWHELMED with a feeling of victory. All day, I claimed this promise, and I made it through the day! I know that this supernatural strength and Providential promise are available and true every single day, but...........

I still found myself sitting here this morning with my mind weighed down by Olivia's illness, my new trimester schedule, early-morning cafeteria duty followed by early-morning backpack-checking duty, a teacher's meeting during my only planning period, and an after-school meeting with literacy specialists from Frankfort..........

Then I opened my Bible.

Yes, I opened my Bible and once again God showed me something that reminded me that even when I feel burdened He has a plan.

In my chronological reading, I am in the book of Numbers. God is instructing Moses about how to set up the tabernacle. Read again what happens in Numbers 7:

When Moses finished setting up the tabernacle, he anointed it and consecrated it and all its furnishings. He also anointed and consecrated the altar and all its utensils. Then the leaders of Israel, the heads of families who were the tribal leaders in charge of those who were counted, made offerings. They brought as their gifts before the LORD six covered carts and twelve oxen-an ox from each leader and a cart from every two. These they presented before the tabernacle.

The LORD said to Moses, "Accept these from them, that they may be used in the work at the Tent of Meeting. Give them to the Levites as each man's work requires."

So Moses took the carts and oxen and gave them to the Levites. He gave two carts and four oxen to the Gershonites, as their work required, and he gave four carts and eight oxen to the Merarites, as their work required. They were all under the direction of Ithamar son of Aaron, the priest. But Moses did not give any to the Kohathites, because they were to carry on their shoulders the holy things, for which they were responsible. When the altar was anointed, the leaders brought their offerings for its dedication and presented them before the altar.

I've read this passage every year for the past four years since Nick died, but I had never been stopped in my tracks while reading about the anointing and consecrating of the tabernacle furnishings like I was this morning.

No, this morning, the Holy Spirit grabbed my attention as if He were saying to me, "Tammy, look at the Kohathites. They were given NOTHING from Moses after the leaders presented their gifts to the Lord." God had specifically said, "Give them (the carts and oxen) to the Levites as each man's work requires." So Moses turned around and gave two carts and four oxen to the Gershonites, four carts and eight oxen to the Merarites, and none to the Kohathites.

WHY?

Scripture gives this reason, "Because the Kohathites were to carry on their shoulders the holy things, for which they were responsible."

I wonder if there was any murmuring among this group as they saw the gifts handed out by Moses.
To be honest, there were exactly enough carts and oxen to be divided equally between all three of these groups, yet Moses specifically gave one group twice as many as another and left the Kohathites to carry on their shoulders the holy things entrusted to them.

Maybe God wants me to be a Kohathite today.

He isn't surprised by what I'm carrying on my shoulders.

He's also not surprised by what you're carrying on yours.

Could it be that God has asked us, much like the Kohathites, to carry some holy things for Him?

Our families, our callings, our gifts...............

I know that today is not going to be easy, but I'm just guessing that the Kohathites may have been tempted to look around and see some unfair use of carts and oxen by other Levites as a reason to complain until they looked up on their shoulders and remembered that God had entrusted them with "holy things."

I opened my Facebook after reading this passage and had an inbox message from a girl who I had taught 6 years ago in 6th grade. She is now a senior at a school in another district and wondered if I remembered her. She said she needed to talk. She asked if I could help her decide about a career choice she is considering. I remember this sweet girl so clearly. She was such a special student to have in class.

Holy things.

God reminded me this morning that the burden I feel on my shoulders is a privilege and an honor.

Olivia and my students........

He has entrusted me to carry them today.

So, with a deep breath, a smile, and the refusal to look around at others who might be getting the help of a cart or an ox, I will do my tasks with the spirit of a Kohathite.

As a Kohathite carried holy things on his shoulders, I will carry my family and my students on mine.

Thankful today for the weight on my shoulders and thankful I could not sleep........I now have a little extra time to get some things done for my "holy things."

What is burdening you today? Is something causing you not to sleep well?

Family, work, grief, loneliness, illness?

Could it be that God has asked you to carry some holy things for His glory?

REFLECTION TIME:

The Bible says that the Lord is close to the brokenhearted. That means God draws near to those who are grieving. He understands the burden that has been placed on your shoulders as you walk the road of grief. He not only understands but also sees your grief as a holy thing. What can you do today as you carry your grief so that God receives glory for His presence in your anguish? Take a few minutes to write about how you are feeling as you travel the road of grief and then ask God to help you carry your grief with the same willingness the Kohathites had as they carried their holy things for Him.

_____

_____

_____

_____

_____

_____

_____

_____

_____

_____

_____

_____

When Life Has Shattered

II Cor. 4:6
For God, who said, "Let light shine out of darkness,"
made his light shine in our hearts to give us the light of the
knowledge of God's glory displayed in the face of Christ.

Wrapped in frail and molded glass, edges scalloped so,
Light has such an easy task of casting a soft glow.

But what happens when life shatters,
breaking promises and dreams?

How do we bounce back and survive
the devil's wicked schemes?

From every angle, it is clear---

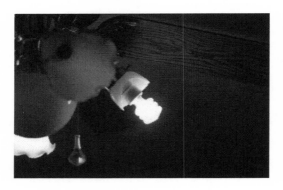

What we once had is gone.

It doesn't take a well-trained eye
to see we're barely hanging on.

Yet as we try to make some sense of all our loss and pain,
We realize that our light is shining brightly just the same.
And maybe in some special way
our glow seems much more bright,
When the wrappings of this world are gone
and all we have is
Light.

So, if you're barely hanging on,
and dreams have seemed to shatter....
Know that you are not alone
And to His heart you matter.

Keep burning for Him through your tears,
Keep lighting up the way.
He promises that joy will come
again to you one day.

And as you shine through brokenness, you're lighting up the
road,
For others who have felt great loss or carry a tough load.

So what happens when life shatters?
Let me tell you what I think,
I think we find out what's beneath the pretty outside shell,
Deep inside our inner self ---
Who does really dwell?

(Thank you, Olivia, for tossing your blanket over the couch
in such a way that the light globe shattered without harming
the bulb.)

REFLECTION TIME:

Do you feel as if from every angle the world can see that part of you is gone? Do you feel unprotected, broken, and frail? Tell God exactly how you feel today.
Ask Him to help you see the beauty in your shattered spirit. Ask Him to help you shine brightly even through your brokenness. Maybe write a poem about your brokenness and see how God speaks to you through this part of life.

_____

_____

_____

_____

_____

_____

_____

_____

_____

_____

_____

_____

_____

Feeling Broken and Whole at the Same Time

Colossians 1:17
He is before all things, and in him all things hold together.

A friend and I were sitting on her porch one evening recently
when another friend from our church family drove by and
asked if we could please help find her dog, Ollie.
Her gate had been left open, and he had escaped!
Before we knew it, we were in my car driving around town
with the windows down shouting, "Ollie, Come here, Ollie!"
Turning down road after road, we began to laugh thinking,
"How did this happen? How did our evening evolve from a
peaceful porch visit to a frantic dog search?"
Little did we know the adventure of the night was just
beginning and a huge part of my grief journey was going to
come to a peaceful end.
Honestly, Ollie's attempt at freedom became the door to
mine.

After driving up and down several roads, Vicki and I ended
up in an alley where several families were setting up for a
yard sale.

I rolled down my window to ask if they had seen a brown boxer to which they replied, "He was here just five minutes ago."
As I was talking to them, I spotted a lamp on one of their tables that looked pretty.
I hopped out of the car to look at it while Vicki was laughing at me from the car.
I looked at the lady who was pricing the items and said, "I really like this lamp. We'll be back!"

After Ollie was finally found on Main Street, Vicki and I hugged Trish (Ollie's owner) and headed back to our surprise Wednesday night yard sale (Who has yard sales in the middle of the week anyway?)
The lamp was only $2, so I made my first purchase.
Then a wooden sign caught my eye!
I have a teacher-friend named Angel,
and I thought this plaque with her name would be a perfect gift to hang by her desk.

I never dreamed just how angelic my night would become, however!

I found a basket that I liked and was fairly sure I had seen everything that interested me.

Then this box caught my eye............

Lying in the box were several pieces to a Nativity set and under them were more wrapped pieces.
I looked at Vicki and said, "I have to buy this!"
(I have a special connection with Nativity sets.........
Partly because the night before Nick passed away Mom and I watched the movie "The Nativity" as Nick lay sleeping on the couch right behind us,
and partly because Nick's death gave me an entirely different perspective of the Nativity scene's message to grieving moms.
Before Nick passed away I had always looked at my Nativity sets as a "group event" focused on Jesus in the manger.
I had never really stopped and looked at each part of the Nativity scene in such a personal away, wondering how each character and animal responded to the birth of baby Jesus.
After Nick's death, my Nativity sets began to reflect Jesus' entire life journey from his birth to his death - especially as I looked at Mary and remembered how God had called her "blessed among women" even when He knew that one day she would kneel at the cross and watch her son die a horrific death.)
As we were leaving the yard sale, I was talking with Vicki about how Mary has become so special to me.

Her life story reminds me that God's definition of "blessed"
isn't always the same as ours.

When I got home later that evening, I began unwrapping
each piece of the set to see what was hidden beneath the
newspaper.

The beauty of each piece took my breath away.

Baby Jesus was even positioned in the manger in such a way
that his arms and feet seemed to foreshadow the position he
would one day be in as he hung on the cross.

I couldn't believe all of these pieces had fit in one not-so-big
box.

And then, as I sat all the pieces out across the coffee table,
Tim noticed that Mary's hands were missing.......
broken and gone.......

This was the only part of this beautiful glass set that wasn't perfect.
I knew at that very moment God was trying to tell me something, but I couldn't quite figure out what it could be.

I kept digging, hoping for more information.
Curious about how long this Nativity set had been wrapped away, I began looking for a date on the newspaper that had carefully held each glass figurine.,

My heart stopped as I read the date, December 24, 1995, in the corner of the newspaper. This was the year Nick was born and the date of his first Christmas Eve.

Seventeen years ago as I held my new baby son someone in Lexington, Kentucky, had wrapped up this Nativity set, and God has been saving it for me ever since.
I texted Trish to see if she was awake and when she replied, "Yes," I called to be sure she wasn't upset with Ollie for running away.

I told her with a smile that I really thought Nick had let him go so I would find this yard sale.
Then I told her the story of the Nativity set and the newspaper date.
She couldn't believe it!
As we were talking, I told her about Mary's hands being gone and I said, "Maybe God is saying, "Let go, Tammy. It's okay."
I really didn't like the thought of God saying this to me, though.
The words "let go" seemed so final.

We got off the phone, and I went back down to sit and look through the old newspaper.
I still felt as if God had something to tell me.
I felt like I was continuing to unwrap a mystery.
Then I found pages in the newspaper wrapping filled with photographs of other children born in 1995.
These pages were entitled,
"Special Christmas Angels."

I knew God was saying, "Tammy, your sweet Nick had his first Christmas in 1995, and now he is a special Christmas angel."

I was speechless.

I slowly took out each piece of newspaper and pressed it down, folding it so that I could save it forever.
And in the middle of one of the sheets of paper I found this...........

Mary's hands!!!!!!!!!!!!!!!!!!!

I set the hands by the Nativity set and took several pictures.

I wanted to somehow show the brokenness of Mary.
I wanted to photograph the cost of being the mother of Jesus, the one called by God to love and then let go.

As I was snapping the photos, my phone vibrated.
I received a text.
Trish (the owner of the dog we had chased and the only friend I think would have remembered what happened in the spring right after Nick passed away) had texted me after thinking about Mary's missing hands and what they could mean.
She remembered my story from Sunday school three years ago, and I believe that is why it was HER DOG who we chased and who eventually led us to the yard sale where I found the Nativity set.

Her text then brought everything from the evening together.
The lost Ollie.
The yard sale.
The Nativity set.
The date on the newspaper.
The broken Mary.
The thought of "letting go" seeming too cold, too difficult, too impossible.
The longing to not be broken yet the realization that there would never be a way to be the "old me" again.

Her text simply said,
"Remember when Beth Moore told you, "You will be whole!"
I did remember!
I remembered Beth praying over me as I wept.
I remembered her holding my chin in her hands as she looked me straight in the eyes and said,
"I prophecy in the name of Jesus, you will be whole! You will be whole!"
I remembered how the words had given me hope.
I remembered how the words had given me strength.
But I also remembered how the words had made me scared.
Scared that in becoming whole I would somehow forget Nick, forget Adrienne, forget what it feels like to grieve.
As I read Trish's text again, I looked back down at Mary.
I looked at her missing hands.
I looked at the pair of hands sitting beside her.
And I lifted them up.
I held them in place.

And suddenly I knew!!!!!!!!!!!!!!!!!!!!!!!

I can be whole and broken at the same time,
if I just let God hold me together!

I thought of the verse in Colossians that says,
He is before all things, and in him all
things hold together.
Because of Him I can be whole while remaining broken.

Maybe, just maybe, God doesn't say "let go" when we lose
someone we love.
Maybe He says, "Let me help you hold on."

I write this rather long devotional, because I want you to
know and believe that GOD IS ALWAYS WORKING!
Maybe it's in the search for a lost dog, a yard sale purchase,
the wrapping of newspaper around a glass object, or broken
figurines.........................
Whatever it may be, GOD IS ALWAYS AT WORK!.
Know today that your yesterdays and your tomorrows are
already being connected in beautiful ways.

You may not understand why things have happened the way
they have (I know I don't),
and in your wildest dreams you may never predict where and
how your life events will connect.
But rest in this knowledge,
"God knows."

And that's all that really matters.

REFLECTION TIME:

Have you ever experienced something you knew could only be orchestrated by the hand of God? If so, take a few minutes to write it out so you'll never forget the details and the emotions of this memory. If not, ask God to help your eyes and ears be open to His messages. Your message may come through a special sunrise, a uniquely-shaped cloud, or a crack in a sidewalk.

No matter how He speaks to you, know and believe that He longs to comfort you and give you hope! Trust Him today with your doubts, fears, and questions. He is already ahead of you creating special ways of letting you know you are loved.

_____

_____

_____

_____

_____

_____

_____

_____

_____

_____

Needing the Great Physician

Jeremiah 29:13
You will seek me and find me when you seek me with all
your heart.

I love my doctor.
I really do.
But I don't always love sitting in a waiting room and paying
my co-pay.
So, when I discovered I had poison ivy a couple of weeks
ago, I decided to take matters into my own hands.
I bought some anti-itch cream at the drug store. Yes, I bought
generic. I read the label and the percentage of active
ingredient in this tube was identical to that in the name
brand..

I "tried" to avoid itching my rash over the next few days, because I didn't want it to spread. Sometimes it wasn't that easy, though, and I forgot.

The poison ivy quickly spread.

I "tried" to avoid going into areas that could have more poison ivy; but when the puppies were getting through the fence at the top of our hill, I decided to try to fix the problem myself and climbed the hill with leftover lattice from our porch and a few zip-ties.

I found the suspicious openings and fastened the lattice tightly so that the puppies couldn't push through the bottom of the fence.

There's something about vines growing through the fence that you're holding onto tightly that should scream, "Watch out!! I could be dangerous!"

But I didn't hear them screaming and kept moving along the fence line, zip-tying as I went!

(I remember riding around in the pick-up with my grandpa on his farm in Oklahoma and watching him "fix fence," but I don't recall him ever using zip-ties. I think cattle are a little stronger than Dash and Domino; but as I think of Grandpa this morning, I'm thinking surely he was proud of me for trying to fix a fence! If only I'd worn gloves and long sleeves, which Grandpa always did!)

Well, needless to say, my poison ivy spread even more this week.

From my right leg to my left leg to my left arm and even to my stomach!

I'd like to say that the quickly spreading poison ivy pushed me to go to my doctor immediately, but I can't.

Instead I went to Family Dollar to pick up some puppy treats and shampoo and asked the manager if he knew of any poison ivy secrets.
He immediately hollered to another employee who appeared from behind a shelf with a wealth of information.

"You need to put apple cider vinegar on every itchy spot; then go to the poison ivy plant and look around it, because near every poisonous plant, grows the cure!!"
He then explained that I needed to find a long-stemmed plant with one orange, bell-shaped flower on top and boil the stems until they were mushy.
Then I was to apply this mushy substance to the affected areas and my poison ivy would go away.

I went home and immediately applied apple cider vinegar to all my itchy spots.
I then climbed my hill in flip-flops (never a great idea) to search for this miracle plant. No luck.

Later in the day, I drove Peppy to a little town outside of Grayson to get his summer haircut. The sweet lady who cuts his hair is full of wisdom, so I said, "Look at my arm!" She immediately reached into a cupboard in her little store and handed me a bottle of honey. "Rub this on every area that is itching. Take a cotton ball and dip it in cool water and then dab the areas to take away the stickiness."

As I drove home with my honey, I was almost laughing at myself......almost.........
When suddenly I looked out my window and noticed long-stemmed plants growing all through the ditch with a single bell-shaped orange flower growing atop the stem!
I pulled into the nearest driveway and turned around, trying to find a place to pull over and get some of the flowers.

When I realized there was no safe place to pull over, I turned onto a side road and into the driveway of a trailer that had these same flowers growing in the ditch right beside it.

I sat for a minute wondering, "What will these people do if they see me in their ditch picking flowers?"
On top of everything, I was in my swimming suit with a cover-up on because I had left a friend at my house by the pool thinking I would be right back!

As I sat in the driveway, a lady opened the door of the trailer to see why I was sitting there.

I got out of the car and quickly said, "You probably wonder why I'm here, but I have a crazy question." She replied, "I may have a crazy answer." She did.

I explained about being covered in poison ivy and about the man at Family Dollar telling me about a particular plant that happened to be growing in her ditch.
She then walked to me, showed me her arm which was obviously in its own poison ivy-recovery mode and went on to say that the only thing that she had had luck with was Lava soap.

The next think I knew, she was back in her trailer getting me a brand new bar of soap!

She then helped me pick some flowers.

I wish you could have seen my friend's face when I returned 40 minutes later with all of this:

Well, I'm going to be honest.
I never boiled the stems.
And I have yet to rub the honey on my body, but we did eat
some of it for dinner and it's delicious!

I did, however, dip the bar of soap in my pool and begin
rubbing it on my arms and legs.

I felt a little like an Appalachian Bathsheba bathing at the
pool, but I promise I was wearing a very modest one - piece
suit with a skirt; and if David had been next door, he never
would have requested my presence in his palace.....ever.

By now, I was officially laughing at myself.

Later that evening, I walked with another friend and told her
my story. After we walked, she looked in her medicine
cabinet and found yet another poison ivy solution, an anti-
itch lotion that was almost to expire, and said,
"Here, use this!"

It did get me through the night!
The next day my poison ivy seemed to be reaching a point of no return, and I bit the bullet and spent several hours in the waiting room of my doctor's office as a walk-in patient. Why does this look so much less inviting than walking through the woods looking for a mysterious flower?

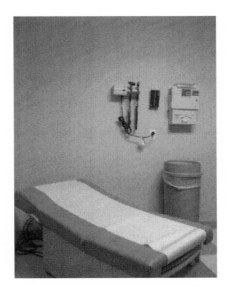

I told her the whole story. One thing I have learned to do is be honest when facing a doctor. You never know if they have a Lava soap detector in the room, so there's no since taking a chance.

She offered to give me a shot and medicine, and my husband still can't believe I opted for only medicine. I truly hate needles, and when she said it would only speed my recovery by about a day; I decided it was worth one more day of agony to avoid a shot. He thinks I'm crazy, but why should I change now?

Anyway, I am on the road to recovery......finally........and I'm thinking all of the tips I received along the way probably do help in mild cases. I just started asking for help a little too late.

Don't we do that in life when we have a problem?

We try to fix it ourselves first?

Then when it gets out of hand, we turn to friends and even strangers for advice, counsel, and help.

Finally, we realize that only the Great Physician has the answer.

So we force ourselves to wait until He provides the help we need.

In the waiting, we always learn something.

Patience, humility, trust, dependence on Someone greater than us.......

Today, you may not have poison ivy, but maybe there's something you're dealing with that seems overwhelming.

Maybe you've tried to fix it.

Maybe you've even turned to friends.

And strangers.

I'm challenging you today to turn to God.

He is patiently waiting to take your problem and deal with it.........

but here's the most difficult part of doing this.

Remember He deals with things in HIS TIME.

Not ours.

234

As you wait for His help, thank Him for the opportunity to grow more patient and the chance to learn more about trusting in Him and Him alone.

II Chron. 15:3-4 says
,
"For a long time Israel was without the true God, without a priest to teach, and without the Law to instruct them.
But whenever they were in trouble and turned to the Lord, the God of Israel, and sought Him out, they found Him."

I love that the Bible speaks to every situation in our lives.
Turn to Him today.
Seek Him.
You will find Him.

Remember Jeremiah 29:13,

You will seek me and find me when you seek me with all your heart.

REFLECTION TIME:

Do you ever feel as if you are turning everywhere for answers to your questions, but your problems either stay the same or continue to get worse? There's something about reaching the point where there is nowhere else to turn but to God that can transform everything about your situation. God longs to be your answer. Talk to Him today about everything that is on your heart. He can handle your anger, your fear, your doubts, your questions. Turn to Him today.

_____

_____

_____

_____

_____

_____

_____

_____

_____

_____

_____

_____

When Time is Not Healing Your Pain

Romans 8:38-39
For I am convinced that neither death nor life, neither angels
nor demons, neither the present nor the future,
nor any power, neither height nor depth, nor anything else in
all creation, will be able to separate us from the love of God
that is in Christ Jesus our Lord.

I never thought that cleaning out my email inbox would leave
me in tears.
But there's something about going back in time that makes
you painfully aware of just how far you have come.
In the days just following Nick's death in 2008, my inbox
was flooded with words of love and sympathy.
I read many of these messages in the first few weeks after
Nick's passing, but time slipped away leaving many of these
powerful notes unopened.
Today, I sat and read words from special alumni at KCU,
Nick's oncologist nurse practitioner, and many more
wonderful friends and family -
new words to me, but words that blessed me today more
deeply than they would have three and a half years ago.

So much time has passed since saying "bye" to Nick, but the
memories of that last season with him are as painfully real
today as they were then.

Grief doesn't go away.

The phrase, "time heals," is a phrase I have heard spoken many times over the years, and I guess it carries a little truth. But I just don't believe time truly heals a deep and painful loss.

The closest I can get to interpreting that phrase in a way that works for me is by saying, "time softens."

Time softens the heartache so that you can smile again, laugh again, even make plans again.

Time softens the memories so that they become sweeter - not so piercingly painful.

Time softens the feelings of panic, fear, regret, sadness.

But grief will always be my companion.

I don't think a mom is ever the same after losing a child.

Yesterday in church, I was smiling as I was singing during worship, and suddenly these questions popped into my mind, "Does anyone see me smile as I sing and doubt my love for my children who are gone? Could anyone possibly think I don't miss Nick and Adrienne? Do I send a message that I am okay with what I have been through?"

On one hand, faith and hope have strengthened me to face my life as it now is.

On the other hand, I am still a frail, hurting mom who truly lives one little day at a time.

God must have placed those thoughts in my mind yesterday during worship, because He knew I would be cleaning my inbox today.

He wanted me to remember today that yesterday I was praising Him with a smile, so that after reading all of these touching notes from 2008, I would believe without a doubt that I would smile again.

At the same time, He knew today would remind me of just how deeply my heart still aches for the presence of my precious Nick. I still miss him more than words could ever say.

Thankful today for Romans 8:38-39 in an extra-powerful way:

For I am convinced that neither
death nor life,
neither angels nor demons,
neither the present nor the future,
nor any powers,
neither height nor depth,
nor anything else in all creation,
will be able to separate us from the
love of God that is in Christ Jesus
our Lord.

REFLECTION TIME:

Has anyone ever tried to comfort you with the words, "Time heals." How did those words make you feel? What has the passing of time done for you in your grief? How would you comfort someone today who was facing a recent loss? Take a few minutes to talk to God about where you are in your grief journey. Ask Him to help soften the pain as time passes. Trust Him to carry you as you face each new day in your heartache.

_____

_____

_____

_____

_____

_____

_____

_____

_____

_____

_____

_____

_____

Ready to Stop Asking, "Why?"

Proverbs 20:24
A person's steps are directed by the LORD. How then can anyone understand their own way?

Sitting in the jail cell last night listening to the inmates talk about their upcoming court dates and the sentences they are expecting, I felt their fear.
Although not bound by visible shackles, they are bound by cinderblock walls and doors with electric locks.
They are bound by past mistakes, present consequences, and future long-term sentencings.

Life without faith is so much like physical imprisonment.

We are trapped in our doubt, our pain, and our questions.

Bound to only what we can see around us.
Short-sighted living.
No hope.

I couldn't make it through today without hope.
The hope of Heaven.
The hope of eternity with Him.
The hope of eternity with so many I love and miss.
Hope keeps me going.

I know I wouldn't have this hope without faith in a Father who isn't shocked by my questions, my struggles, my mistakes.

I love that no matter what today or tomorrow holds, God is already there in the midst of them working in ways only He can work.
He's working in your life today, too.

He's not wringing His hands in worry or regret as He watches the nightly news, wondering why He created this world in the first place.
No, He has a big plan, a big purpose.

In spite of all the bad news and bad people, He can bring good.

There's something very freeing about reaching a point in your walk with God when you can honestly say, "I don't understand Your plan, Lord, but I've stopped trying to figure it out."

Reaching this place in our faith walk frees us -
Frees us to trust that we have a Father who is sitting on His throne, relaxed and in control.

As you walk through your day, remember that even when you are not aware of it, the Lord is directing your every step when you allow Him to walk with you.
Take a deep breath and lean back into His arms.

"He's got this!"

The New Living Translation of Proverbs 20:24 says,
"The Lord directs our steps, so why try to understand everything along the way?"

REFLECTION TIME:

Are you at a place in your grief where you feel freed from your questions or are you still asking God, "Why?" No matter where you are in your grief journey, God is there. He can handle your questions. He can also release you from them when you are ready. Talk to Him today about how you feel. Ask Him to cover your doubt with His mercy and your struggles with His peace.

_____

_____

_____

_____

_____

_____

_____

_____

_____

_____

_____

_____

Longing to See What He Sees

Other than a face you can somewhat make out in the side of
it if you look at it just right,
there's nothing spectacular about the little hill in Jerusalem
referred to as, "Golgotha, The Place of the Skull."
(Matt. 27:33)

It's just a little, rocky hill in a country far away from the one
in which I live.

It's one of thousands, probably millions, of hills I'll never see
in my lifetime.

I'd like to see it, though.

I'd like to climb to the top and see the view.

In human terms, it's just a place called Golgotha, but to many
it's a popular tourist attraction.

Why has a rocky, little hill in a tiny country continued to
draw crowds for years and years?

I think I know why.

I think deep inside every human heart there is the longing to know and believe that something happened on that hill that made
every unfair life experience,
every unanswerable question,
every doubt,
every fear,
every unanswered prayer.........
become bearable.

On that hill, Jesus died.
And three days later He rose again.

Even those who don't believe are drawn here just to see this place.
Just to see firsthand the location that Christians claim and history points to as the very spot where Jesus willingly died for me and for you.

I've struggled lately with unanswered prayers from the past.
I've questioned why God doesn't give everyone a miracle when they need one.
I've felt a little blue and a little guilty at the same time.

Last night as I was at worship at KCU, the song leader was sharing about the unbelievable power of the Creator of the Universe and something flooded over me.

I saw Jesus on the cross and for the first time I realized just how difficult it must have been for God to withhold His Hand from those who were killing His Son.

To have all the power of the universe at your disposal and choose to watch Your Son die for many who would reject Him.

WHY? Why would God do this?

I asked myself this question in my head over and over last night as I stood in worship and I finally received the answer.

God KNEW this was the only way to open the door to Heaven and forgiveness and life with Him eternally once and for all.

God knew this was the only way to conquer death.

He saw the other side.
He saw Sunday while we saw Friday.
He saw glorious resurrection while we saw painful agony.

And then I saw Nick in my mind.
Nick, weak and so beaten down by cancer.
Nick, frail to the point of needing help to painfully move from his wheelchair to the couch.
Nick, no longer able to use his arm and hand.
Nick, no longer able to smile.

Then I saw God looking down and holding back the power to heal.
Suddenly I realized that God had heard our prayers and had made the choice NOT to heal Nick.
His answer was not the answer we longed for, but it was His answer.
It must have been difficult.
He must have wanted to heal Nick so badly.

As I cried in my heart and still begged, "WHY!?!?!"
I knew the truth.

God saw the other side.
God saw Sunday while we saw Friday.

He saw glorious resurrection for Nick while we saw painful agony.

I believe God knew that through Nick's death many other grieving moms and dads would find life and hope.
Nick's victory came through death.
Our family's ministry came through our hope and belief in the resurrection.

My prayer today is that I can come to grips with my grief and that Nick's death will continue to be a light to others who do not receive an earthly miracle.
I cling to verses like Romans 8:18.

I cling to the Hope of Heaven.

I miss Nick so much.
I could not take another step in this world if I did not believe with all my heart that I am walking on the road to Golgotha daily.

The high, but painful road.

On this road I am promised that these present sufferings cannot compare to the glory I will one day see.
Thank you, Lord, for this promise!

REFLECTION TIME:

Does the pain in your life ever leave you wondering where God is? I find great comfort in knowing that as His own Son died on the cross God was already seeing the glory of His coming resurrection. God sees what we can't see too. He sees Sunday while we see Friday. Today, ask Him to give you a glimpse of Sunday. Ask Him to fill you with the power of the resurrection and a deep belief that your present sufferings cannot compare to the glory you will one day see!

_____

_____

_____

_____

_____

_____

_____

_____

_____

_____

_____

_____

FACING DAWN

Trusting God as He Writes Your Story

Hebrews 12:1-2

Therefore, since we have so great a cloud of witnesses
surrounding us, let us also lay aside every encumbrance and
the sin which so easily entangles us, and let us run
with endurance the race that is set before us, fixing our eyes
on Jesus, the author and perfecter of faith,
who for the joy set before Him endured the cross, despising
the shame, and has sat down at the right hand of the throne
of God.

Recently I picked up the book, "**EPIC: The Story God is
Telling and the Role That is Yours to Play**," by John
Eldredge. (Thomas Nelson Publishing, 2007)

Immediately, I knew this book was going to be "just what I
needed" as I read the quote by G.K. Chesterton at the
beginning,

*"I had always felt life first as a story and if there is a story
there is a story teller."*

I love this quote, because it reminds me of conversations
with my sister as we were growing up.

When a big event in life would come to a close, we would often say,
"Well, I guess it's time to start a new chapter."

When something big was about to happen, we would ask each other, "I wonder what will happen in this chapter?"

Even though I wasn't reading many books during those young years of my life, God was writing my life into a story.

As I read Eldredge's first chapter, I was reminded that God continues to write my story even as I'm grieving just as He continues to write yours.

My Bible reading this morning included the story of Mary coming to the well and meeting Jesus there.
If you've read this story you know that Mary had experienced some pretty rough chapters in her life, and even at this moment was living in sin with a man who wasn't her husband.
Her story was one that I am sure she was ashamed of, and meeting Jesus at the well was not the chapter she was expecting to be entering as she arrived at the well.
Just like Mary, we never know when a new chapter in life is beginning..
It almost brings tears to my eyes when I think of how critical this moment was in Mary's life story.
After her conversation with a Man she has never met, Mary's life changes forever.
She goes from sinner to redeemed, hopeless to hope-full, lost to found, forsaken to loved, used to cherished.
The path she took to get to the well and to this life-changing moment was a path she walked nearly every day.
I don't know about you, but I feel a kind-of excitement this morning when I remember that God is always working.

Even when we feel that life is mundane and hopeless, God is penning the next words, the next pivotal moment.

Maybe your job is miserable.
Maybe your marriage is falling apart.
Maybe you have been making really bad decisions.
Maybe you're lonely.
Maybe you're sad.
Maybe you're heart is broken.
No matter how you find yourself today, remember this,

Jesus longs to show up on your everyday path and transform your life story.

Even in our grief, God holds the pen, using every tear and every heartache to move our life story towards His love. Like a movie director who sets the stage perfectly so that a powerful drama can unfold, God looks at you and says, "I want your story to mean something!"

REFLECTION TIME:

Does the thought of God writing your story bring you comfort or make you feel angry? Tell God how you feel about the story He is writing with your life. Ask Him to help you find peace in your life story even when it's difficult. Allow God to use your grief to draw you closer to Him while pushing you out into a hurting world filled with people who need to hear the story of God's unfailing love. Write your own story out into a journal, asking God to show you how He has been working all along the way.

_____

_____

_____

_____

_____

_____

_____

_____

_____

_____

_____

_____

_____

When God's Teachings Are Hard

As I read the Bible this morning, I wouldn't have predicted
stumbling across a moment in Jesus' life that really bothers
me.
I've read this particular story many times.
Actually, I remember writing about this very passage several
years ago when we were praying for Nick's healing.
I remember telling God over and over again that I believed
He could move the mountain of Nick's cancer.
I believed without a doubt to the very last day of Nick's life
that God could heal him completely.
So, this morning as I read the passage where Jesus caused the
fig tree to wither and then turned to the disciples and said,
"You can pray for anything, and if you have faith, you will
receive it,"
my heart sunk.........all over again.

Questions ran through my mind just like they did in the
months following Nick's death.

Did I have enough faith?
Did God hear our prayers?
Did I do something wrong?
Did I have unforgiveness in my heart toward anyone?
Was there a sin in my life that was blocking my prayers?

On and on and on and on.............questions darted through my mind.

It would be easy to throw in the towel sometimes and just say, "This religion stuff doesn't make sense."
But there are several reasons why I never will.

First, throwing in the towel wouldn't bring Nick back. It would actually put me in a place of no hope, no future, no promise of seeing him again.
Second, even Jesus prayed for his "cup to be removed" when the cross became a very-near reality.
Yes, Jesus prayed in faith that God would not make Him endure the pain of the crucifixion, but we know He did not receive the answer He desired.
Third, Paul prayed for a thorn to be removed from his flesh, and the answer he received was "my grace is sufficient for you."
I know Paul had great faith, and yet his prayer was not answered in the way he wanted either.
Fourth, I prayed for Nick's complete healing when he was sick; and that is exactly what he received. Earthly healing is temporary. Pain and death still await all who are healed while they are on this planet. Even the people Jesus healed eventually passed away. So, if I think clearly and logically, my prayer was answered completely.

Today, if you stumble upon hard teachings, don't throw in the towel.

Remember, there is a bigger picture than today.

Trust God even when His teachings are hard.

REFLECTION TIME:

As you walk the road of grief, do you find yourself stumbling over certain parts of the Bible? Are there stories that confuse you or make you upset? Tell God how you feel. Ask Him to help you understand what you can learn from these hard teaching? Ask Him to help you trust Him even when it's difficult.

_____

_____

_____

_____

_____

_____

_____

_____

_____

_____

_____

_____

_____

_____

_____

FACING DAWN

Years After Grief Began

PSALM 40:1-3

I WAITED PATIENTLY FOR THE LORD;
HE TURNED TO ME AND HEARD MY CRY.
HE LIFTED ME OUT OF THE SLIMY PIT,
OUT OF THE MUD AND MIRE;
HE SET MY FEET ON A ROCK
AND GAVE ME A FIRM PLACE TO STAND.
HE PUT A NEW SONG IN MY MOUTH,
A HYMN OF PRAISE TO OUR GOD.
MANY WILL SEE AND FEAR
AND PUT THEIR TRUST IN THE LORD.

Sometimes in grief you reach a place of peace and resignation.

That's kind-of where I am with the loss of our infant daughter, Adrienne.

Seeing her tombstone daily for twenty years and realizing that all of my friends' children who were born that same year are now busily completing college and planning weddings,

I sort-of reached a place where I thought maybe Adrienne's short little life had served its biggest purposes in doing these three things:

1. Teaching me deep compassion for the hurting

2. Pushing us to adopt Olivia from India

3. Preparing me for the difficult road of letting Nick go

I had deep peace in knowing that my six-week experience as Adrienne's mom was a gift and that the lessons she taught me would be with me my entire lifetime.

I really never expected anymore until last week when I received a Facebook message from a lady I had never met who recently lost her baby to SIDS and was looking for support.

Just one week later we have a Facebook page for eight moms who have all walked this horrific road of waking to find a child has died in his/her sleep.

Talking with these moms, I realized that the pain I felt twenty years ago was very normal.

I realized that I somehow muddled through grief without a group of women who were walking the same road and it was only by the grace of God that I did not crack.

I came close.

I can remember sitting in a mall parking lot all alone squirting St. John's Wart, an herb for calming nerves, under my tongue and thinking, "This is it. I have lost my mind."

But God had other plans and somehow He pulled me out of a pit and gave me hope and a promise.

As you grieve, I want to encourage you to do these three things.

First, allow yourself time and space for God to work.

Second, thank God for being with you in all those times and spaces.

Third, know that no matter how many years pass by, God longs to use your journey to help others who walk behind you.

REFLECTION TIME:

No matter how far down the road of grief you've walked, moments will arise unexpectedly reminding you of the pain you felt in your early days of heartache. These reminders, while sometimes painful, can also help you reach out to others with the compassion and love of Jesus in a way someone who has never grieved deeply ever could. Take a few minutes to write about your early grief. Ask God to remind you of the feelings you experienced and allow Him to use you to help someone else who is joining you on this painful road.

_____

_____

_____

_____

_____

_____

_____

_____

_____

_____

_____

FACING DAWN

When Life is a Mess

Psalm 40:1-3

> I waited patiently for the LORD;
> And He inclined to me and heard my cry.
> ² He brought me up out of the pit of destruction, out of
> the miry clay,
> And He set my feet upon a rock making my footsteps firm.
> ³ He put a new song in my mouth, a song of praise to our
> God;
> Many will see and fear
> And will trust in the LORD.

She was only five, but she spoke to me in the midst of a classroom full of kindergartners trying to finish a sequencing task.
As one child cried because she didn't know how to use scissors,
this particular brown-eyed, mussed-up-haired child looked up at me and said,
"My finguhs aw stuck togethew."

In the excitement of getting it all right on her test, this sweet little girl had screwed her glue stick right out of its holder.

Trying to shove it back in, she had discovered that squeezing a stick of glue back into its holder is a lot more complicated than getting it out in the first place.

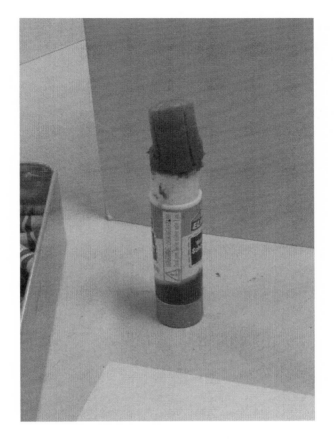

In the midst of trying to solve her own problem, she now had two.

Sticky fingers and an unusable glue stick.

I wanted to sit down and tell this little girl I knew just how she felt.
I wanted to explain in adult terms just how normal she really was because; honestly, I saw my eyes in the eyes of this young child.

I saw someone longing to please, longing to do a good job, and then realizing that in her eagerness to hear the words, "Great job!" she had wound up in a mess.

I want to please God even in my grief.
I want to do well.
I want to demonstrate that I understand exactly what's asked of me,
but sometimes in the excitement of being "all I can be," I find myself overextending my glue stick, leaving me with an empty container and a big mess.

It's hard to restore what I've already emptied.

In the process of trying, I reach tough places much like this little girl........
with my "finguhs stuck togethew."

Suddenly, the task I was trying to complete doesn't seem nearly as urgent as the ungluing of my "finguhs."

Doesn't the devil love when our fingers are stuck together.
We are so unusable.
So unable to even lift our hands in praise.

My mind wandered as I thought of this little girl's predicament, and then I heard her cute little voice saying to her teacher, "Can I go wash my hands?"
She knew what to do when she was stuck.
She turned to her teacher.

I started this week with a list full of tasks,
and I ended this week realizing that sometimes **I** am the most difficult task on my list.
I am the mess.

I am the little girl who extended things too far, trying to
please everyone.
Stuck in a mess.
Needing restored.
At the very same time, I am the glue stick holder.
Emptied.
And difficult to refill.

What do I do when my "finguhs are stuck togethew" and my
glue stick is empty?

That's been the question on my mind this week, even though
I didn't really understand how I was feeling until I stood in a
kindergarten classroom Friday.
It was in this classroom that God showed up and spoke
through a five-year old student.

Isn't that just how God works?
Through children.
Through glue sticks.
Through messes.

He very clearly said to me, "Tammy, I hold all things
together. Your life gets messy when you try to hold it
together with your own strength."

So, I snapped a photo of the messy glue stick as the little girl
watched and grinned.
She wasn't worried about her unfinished sequencing task for
her teacher.
She wasn't even worried about her "finguhs."
She giggled through her mess while I stood beside her, much
older and supposedly much wiser, pondering all the messes
inside of me.

As I turned to walk away, I saw a hanging on the wall that I
read,
"Please excuse the noise and mess-the kids are making happy
memories."

I had read the plaque many times before,
but today it spoke to me.
I saw something new in its words...something I needed to see
in a very personal way. I needed to know that God gets me.
He understands me even when my life is noisy and messy.
He sees me, one of His children, trying to make happy
memories in the midst of a noisy, messy world; and I think
He smiles even when my hands are stuck together.
He smiles when your hands are stuck together too.

Really, it's not so much that we have messes.
It's really what we do when we realize we are stuck.

Do we sit and cry?
Maybe sometimes.

Eventually, though, we realize we only have one option.

No new tasks will be completed before we step away from
our mess and head to a place of cleansing.
And after we're cleansed, we pick up a new glue stick.
Maybe we won't open this one with the same kind of gusto,
but we open it anyway.
Because in the twisting of the glue stick we show the world
that even though life is messy it's worth the risk of sticky
fingers.

I've been emptied this week.

And I've been stuck.

So I'm using this weekend to cleanse myself through some much-needed rest and reflection.

Grief caught me off guard this week and made me a mess..

I think I needed some time with my grief.
It had been a while since I had cried.
My family graciously gave me the space I needed.

I'm sensing it's almost time to wash my face and climb out of this pit for a while, though.

It's time to clean up my mess and get "unstuck."

If you ever find yourself feeling extremely blue or "stuck," know that God understands, He hears your cries, He loves you, and He longs to lift you out of the pit.
Sometimes, He makes you sit there a while, though, with sticky fingers, just so you'll realize how wonderful it is to be rescued and restored!

I'm thankful for a 5 year-old who reminded me that when I'm stuck I need to turn to my Teacher.

REFLECTION TIME:

In your grief, do you ever feel like a mess? Do you ever feel so emptied that you can't imagine how you'll ever be refilled? God understands and loves you even in your messiness and emptiness. He longs to get you out of your mess and fill you back up with His love. Take a few minutes to write about how you are feeling today. Maybe you are the little girl whose fingers are stuck. Maybe you are the glue stick, empty and difficult to fill. Or maybe you are both. No matter what, God cares, understands, and promises to be provide exactly what you need. Don't be afraid to ask Him.

_____

_____

_____

_____

_____

_____

_____

_____

_____

_____

On a Different Road

2 Corinthians 1:3-4
Praise be to the God and Father of our Lord Jesus Christ, the
Father of compassion and the God of all comfort,
who comforts us in all our troubles, so that we can comfort
those in any trouble with the comfort we ourselves have
received from God.

About six months after Nick passed away, I joined an online
support group for parents who have lost children to brain
tumors.
I never really thought I needed a "support group."
However, in the past few years I've learned there's something
very special about a community of people who share the
same struggle.

I'm more of a "reader" than a "writer" when it comes to
participating in this online community, though.
Every once in a while I share a thought or two, but normally I
just read and soak in other people's comments, ideas, and
questions.
Most of the time, I find myself coming up short with any
kind of wisdom.
Probably because I have the same questions, the same fears,
the same kind of tough days.

Over 200 parents belong to this community.

We represent a lot of pain.
We represent a lot of different walks of life.
And we definitely represent a lot of different views of life and death.

But one thing we all have in common is this: we all miss our kids.

That's where I find my bond with these moms, dads, and grandparents.
So last week after I had a scare with my health, I found comfort in the words one mom wrote regarding her daughter's recent struggle with a recurring headache.
She wrote her words in response to another mom's emotional struggle with a child who was having strange headaches.
This is what she said,
"A headache is never "just a headache" anymore for any of us.
It is a trigger to our grief and a reason for anxious thoughts about the terrible thing happening to our family again."

As I sat and read her words, a feeling of "being normal" came over me.
Sometimes in the "real world" I don't feel normal very often.

Conversations happen, in which I am a participant, and words are said that strike me in a totally different way than they do anyone else.
I don't react externally, but internally I often feel the accidental knife.
I feel the reality that there are just some things about me that have separated me from the world's view of normal.

Grief calls people to a higher road of patience, love, and mercy; because when you lose someone you love deeply,

you are shoved up against the frailty of life in a way
unimaginable to your non-grieving friends.
You understand that plans are simply plans.....not promises.
You realize that dates on a calendar can mean celebrations
for one family and agony for another.
You "get" the fact that family pictures never feel quite right
anymore.
You receive Christmas cards that share the joy of the season
and yet you realize that for many the season lacks the joy it
once had.

Not that grieving people never laugh anymore or want to
smile.
Not that grieving people can't let go.
Not that grieving people are hopeless.
They just walk a road parallel to and yet separate from their
non-grieving friends.

Our road crosses over the same events as our non-grieving
friends.
We do birthdays.
We do Christmas.
We do parties.
We do jobs.
But we do everything with an underlying awareness that
something about us is just a little different.

So, for me, even with my extreme confidence in Christ,
even with my deep belief that one day I will hold Adrienne
and hug Nick again in eternity,
I need a support group.

I need to know that there are other moms and dads out there
who are trying to decide how to sign their Christmas cards.

I need to know that there are other families out there who want to keep their children alive in the hearts of their other children and in the hearts of aunts and uncles.

I need to know that other parents are wondering what they can do throughout the holidays to keep their child who is gone present in the love and in the laughter.

I realize I will never be "normal" again when it comes to being a mom.
But last week those words from another grieving mom helped me.
They helped me realize that my recent vision scare was a pretty normal time for me to panic and fear the worst.

As I step back into another Monday, I step back into it thankful.
Thankful for friends who have never walked the road I walk.
But also thankful for friends who walk the same road I do.

REFLECTION TIME:
If you find yourself struggling with any type of problem that isolates you from those around you, I highly recommend finding a support group. Ask God to lead you to a group who will provide the comfort and support you need. If you cannot find a group, consider starting your own. You never know who else is out there who needs just what you need.

_____

_____

_____

_____

_____

_____

_____

_____

_____

_____

_____

_____

_____

FACING DAWN

In an Uncertain World

Romans 8:38-39

For I am convinced that neither death nor life, neither angels
nor demons, neither the present nor the future, nor any
powers,
neither height nor depth, nor anything else in all creation,
will be able to separate us from the love of God that is in
Christ Jesus our Lord.

I woke up this morning with several friends on my mind.

One of my friends faced the unexpected loss of her sister this
past Friday.
Today her family will attempt to step back into a world that
has forever been changed.

Another friend is sitting at the bedside of her mother whose
health is failing quickly.
So many things about this world we live in are uncertain and
painful.

We hold on with a very weak grasp, because truly we are
weak.

As I read the Bible this morning, I read each verse with
hurting friends in mind.

I wondered how the words I read would fall on their aching hearts if they were reading them this morning.

I wondered how God could speak to them today through His promises, and I found great comfort in the words from Romans 8.

Personally, I am wordless today when I think of the fresh pain in the lives of so many people I love.
Nothing I say or do can begin to comfort their hurting hearts.
I'm so thankful for a Bible full of promises and words of hope.

As someone who walks the road of grief daily, I would be lost without God's Word in my life.
I look at my Bible sitting here next to me -
the Bible I have clung to daily since Nick's death four years ago - pages torn, wrinkled, weathered, and stained -
my prayer is that all who are hurting will turn to it with their doubts, their questions, their fears, and their uncertainties.

I do not have the answers for my friends who are hurting, but I know the One who does.

So, today, as I pray for my precious friends with broken hearts and for all who find themselves waking up to an uncertain Monday full of heartache,
I ask God to give them just what they need today and lead them to His Words exactly when they need them.

In an uncertain world, I am thankful for a certain Savior, a certain Lord, and a certain Love from which no power on Heaven or Earth can separate us.
I'm clinging to him who is certain and who loves us deeply and unconditionally through all of our uncertain days.

REFLECTION TIME:

In a world filled with so much sadness, it is easy to become depressed and discouraged, especially when we carry our own grief as well as the grief of others. Who are you hurting for today besides yourself? Take some time to write them a note of encouragement and share a verse or two that has strengthened you along the way. I'm thinking God will use those very verses to bring comfort to your hurting soul too. I just love how He works.

_____

_____

_____

_____

_____

_____

_____

_____

_____

_____

_____

_____

When Your Miracle Didn't Happen

2 Corinthians 1:3-4
Praise be to the God and Father of our Lord Jesus Christ,
the Father of compassion and the God of all comfort,
who comforts us in all our troubles,
so that we can comfort those in any trouble with the
comfort we ourselves receive from God.

Jesus didn't try to hide the truth from His disciples when He
said,
"In this world you will have troubles."

One common thread throughout history is that life has never
been perfectly free from difficult moments for any
generation.

I've questioned God many times in life, wondering why the
Perfect Creator could not create a perfect planet.

Every time I reach these points of questioning, though, I end
up right back where I started.
I am reminded that God's purpose in creating us was not to
display any kind of perfectness outside of Himself.

His purpose was to create a people who would long to be in fellowship with Him.
As someone who has had times of comfort and ease in my life as well as times of trials and heartache,
I can say without hesitation that I am closest to God when I need Him most.

Fellowship with God often begins when we need Him most.

God longs to be our comfort, our Hope, and our strength as we face all of the imperfect moments this world brings.

He longs to teach us just how much He loves us through our sorrow, and grow deep inside of us a longing for and great expectation of all that is to come in eternity when PERFECTION comes to take us all Home.

I believe that in our darkest moments God does His greatest works.

In the world's eyes, physical healings are reasons to say, "It's a miracle!"

In God's eyes, however, Heaven brings the perfect miracle, complete and eternal healing.

When we reach the place in our grief journey, where we can see the miracles that have happened outside of physical healing, we become what the Bible calls "more than conquerors."

We begin to grasp the reality that death cannot separate us from the love of God and that is a miracle in and of itself.

My smile today even as I continue to grieve the loss of two children is a miracle.

My Hope is a miracle.

My faith is a miracle.

My laugh is a miracle.

My ability to say to all of you who are brokenhearted, "You can make it!" is a miracle.

Jesus conquering death is a miracle!

When I read these verses from II Corinthians 1,
I begin to understand exactly what a miracle is.

A miracle is a God who can create an imperfect world full of imperfect people facing imperfect and difficult moments yet place deep inside each of us a longing for eternity and a Hope that can rise out of our pain.

Not just enough Hope to survive,
but a Hope that endures and brings so much comfort that eventually, even in spite of our brokenness, we somehow become vessels of comfort to others who are hurting.

How does God do that?

How does God take broken, hurting people and transform them into encouragers and comfort givers?

I DO NOT KNOW.

But, I do know this,
IT'S A MIRACLE!

So, today, if your earthly miracle didn't happen and you find
yourself with empty arms,
I write to say this,
"The miracle is coming. The miracle is on its way."

Lean on Him today and tomorrow and the next day in your
heartache.
Trust in Him today and tomorrow and the next day in your
sadness and pain.
Turn to the Comforter today and tomorrow and the next day,
and don't be afraid to tell Him just how sad and confused and
angry and broken you are.

One day you'll wake up and find yourself bringing comfort
to a friend,
and you won't even understand how it happened that you, a
frail, hurting, emotionally-overwhelmed human being, could
ever be the source of strength to someone else.

This, my sweet friend, is the greatest earthly miracle.

So, today, I challenge you to praise God even in your
sadness.

Tell Him how you feel, give Him your broken heart, and then
allow Him to start His slow and steady work on you.

One day, your tears will be washed away.
Perfection will come.
Eternity in Heaven will be your past, present, and future.
Until then, I know we'll still have days when we feel
extremely blue and confused.

We'll still cry.
Our hearts will still ache.

But because of our faith in the Father of all Comfort, let's allow Him to be a continual miracle worker in our hearts so that others can know and experience fully how wide and deep and wonderful God's love is.

Ephesians 3:14-19

For this reason I kneel before the Father, from whom every family in heaven and on earth derives its name.
I pray that out of his glorious riches he may strengthen you with power through his Spirit in your inner being,
so that Christ may dwell in your hearts through faith. And I pray that you, being rooted and established in love,
may have power, together with all the Lord's holy people, to grasp how wide and long and high and deep is the love of Christ,
and to know this love that surpasses knowledge-that you may be filled to the measure of all the fullness of God.

REFLECTION TIME:

I still struggle with the fact that we did not receive the miracle of physical healing for Nick; but as the years pass by, I meet more and more people who are hurting just like I am.

I realize that because God has brought me through the darkest valley by using others who have walked the road before me, I must now be a light to those who follow. Make a list of people who have brought you comfort in your pain.

Ask God to use you to be that same kind of comfort to someone else whose heart is broken. Slowly, you will begin to see God working a miracle through you and in you.

_____

_____

_____

_____

_____

_____

_____

_____

_____

_____

_____

_____

Needing an Anchor for Your Soul

Hebrews 6:18-19
God did this so that, by two unchangeable things in which it is impossible for God to lie, we who have fled to take hold of the hope set before us may be greatly encouraged. We have this hope as an anchor for the soul, firm and secure.

Like a ship lost at sea, we can often feel beaten and bruised by the crashing waves of life when we don't have something anchoring us to the shore.

We try to find anchors in our careers, but sometimes jobs are lost.

We try to find anchors in our friends, but often they let us down without even realizing it.

We try to find anchors in our families, but tragedies occur leaving us defenseless and broken.

Whatever we try to hold onto tightly in this world can easily slip through our fingers like sand.

So how do we find an anchor in an uncertain, ever-changing, often scary world?

Hebrews 6 says that God has given both a pledge and an oath, and that these two things are unchangeable.

He assures us that those who receive His promise can be perfectly sure that He will never change His mind.

This means that since He promises Heaven for those who accept His Son as Savior, then Heaven is a guaranteed future for Christians.

Because of this promise, Hebrews goes on to say that those "who have fled to Him for refuge can have great confidence as we hold to the hope that lies before us."

When we have this hope, listen to what we have for our souls...........

"This hope is a strong and trustworthy anchor for our souls. It leads us through the curtain into God's inner sanctuary."

I don't know about you, but I need a sanctuary.
I need a quiet place to know I am in the presence of God.

I need peace.

When storms hit, which they will, know that God has promised an anchor.

This anchor is Hope.

Hope leads us all to the place we long to be:

In God's presence.

If you're needing Him today, know that Hope can lead you there..........

…and keep you there.

Through every storm, every fear, every question, every tear. Jesus led the way, conquered death, paid the price, and set us free.

When He came, He became our anchor.

That's why He's called our Savior.

He saved us.

Turn to Him today.

REFLECTION TIME:

Do you ever feel like a ship being tossed around in the crashing waves of the sea? God longs to throw you the anchor of Hope that comes from knowing His Son as your Savior. The Bible says that this Hope "does not disappoint." (Romans 5:5) If you are tired of feeling disappointed, talk to God today about how you feel. Ask Him to replace your doubts, fears, and anxieties with the confidence that comes from knowing Him personally as your Lord and Savior.

_____

_____

_____

_____

_____

_____

_____

_____

_____

_____

_____

_____

Broken but Willing to be Used

Colossians 1:17
He is before all things, and in him all things hold together.

As a broken person, I am called to broken things.

Like a broken broom, bent to the point of almost breaking but still able to sweep up paper,

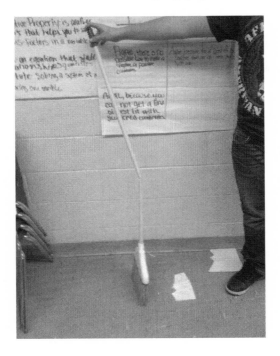

a broken notebook,

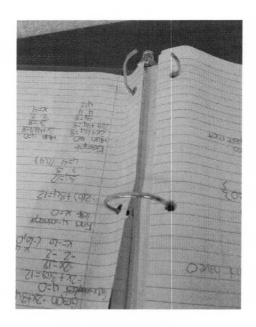

falling apart but still holding a student's papers.

In spite of their condition, I love that they weren't thrown away,
cast aside, or deemed "unworthy" of their original purposes.

Sometimes in my grief I feel like this broom or this notebook.

It's easy to feel incapable of doing any good or making any kind of difference when my heart feels sad and torn apart.

I'm so thankful God promises to hold all things together in this world.
When I hear this promise, I believe there is hope for me.
I believe there might even be a reason for my pain.

I become more and more certain that God still longs to use me.

If you are broken, God longs to hold you together and use you too.

We are valued in His eyes.
We are loved.
We are worthy.
We are still needed.

I'm so thankful God doesn't throw away broken people or people who are falling apart.

No, He does quite the opposite.

Psalm 34:18 promises that God is close to the brokenhearted and saves those who are crushed in spirit.

He doesn't throw us away,

He saves us!!!

Col. 1:17 promises that "He is before all things, and in him all things hold together."

He doesn't abandon us in our brokenness,

He holds us together!!!!!!!!!!!

Today, lean back in these promises and know that God loves you and still longs to use you......
through your brokenness and your pain.

REFLECTION TIME:

Like me, do you ever feel like a broken broom or an almost-useless notebook? What are you longing to do for God but struggling to find the energy, the courage, or the strength to do? Talk to Him about your dreams. Ask Him to use you today even in your brokenness.

_____

_____

_____

_____

_____

_____

_____

_____

_____

_____

_____

FACING DAWN

It Is What It Is...but SO IS HE!

John 14:27
"I am leaving you with a gift—peace of mind and heart.

And the peace I give **is** a gift the world cannot give. So don't be troubled or afraid. (NLT)

I've been called to some hard places in life just like you.
I could question, argue, whine, complain, and doubt all day long every day.
I could choose to let this be it.
My destiny could be wrapped up in, "She's lost two children, poor thing."
But, there's something about choosing to walk right next to Jesus in your grief that wipes all the "poor thingness" away.
You just can't walk close to a King and feel poor or pitiful.
So, as I was facing another tough day last Saturday when Maria moved out of our house and left us with yet another empty room,
I knew there had to be significance in the spilling of all these magnetic words from a box I was moving.
I've learned that when you walk close to God He speaks through spills and sunsets, and everything in between.

I snapped a picture and went on with my work, wondering what in the world God would say through this.

As I walked through the room later that evening after cleaning up most everything and getting the room all organized, I noticed a black square on the carpet.
I turned the little square over and was struck by the word on this one little magnet that had remained unseen and unmoved in my clean up earlier.

Who knew two letters could mean so much to me at this very moment?
As I looked at the word, "is," I couldn't help but think,
"It is what it is."
Life **is** tough.
Life **is** often hard to understand.
Life hurts.
Life can be confusing.
Life **is** a series of "hellos" and "goodbyes" and "see you soons."
Life **is** what we make it.
So, I decided to keep that "**is**" out of the box of words and laid it on my desk,
because I didn't want to forget that moment of being alone in a room that was causing my heart to feel sad and know that God was saying,
It **IS** okay.
It **IS** part of my plan.
It **IS** what you make it.
And so, I've thought a lot about the word "**is**" in the past five days,
and I've realized that while life "**is**" so many different things all rolled into one,
God **IS** so much more.
Today, if you feel like life **IS** difficult.
Remember, God **IS** with you.
He **is** alive.
He **is** aware of your struggle.
He **is** there when no one else is.
He **is** a good listener.
And on and on and on..........

Today, you may find yourself feeling very good about all the things that life **is**......
I HOPE YOU ARE!!!!!!!!!!!!!!

But even in those good times, never forget that God **IS** pursuing you always.

He **IS** passionate about your soul.

He **IS** working every day to bring you closer and closer to Him.

He **is** relentless.

He **is** always there for you.

I'm thankful for a spilled box of magnetic letters.

I'm especially thankful that "**IS**" didn't make it back into the box!!

The great "I AM" spoke to me through the small word "**is**."

I love that about God!!

The Creator of the Universe, who could get our attention every day with majestic fireworks in the sky if He so desired, chooses to speak in small ways.

So, today, be listening, looking, watching, and waiting for Him to show up.

Even if it's in a tiny word like "**is**" spilled right out onto your floor.

Look carefully, it may be turned upside down and just waiting for you to notice!

Have a wonderful day and know that God **IS** with you!

REFLECTION TIME:
As you face another day in your grief, take a few minutes to write down all the ways God **IS** present in your pain. If you cannot think of anything to write, take a few minutes to ask God to show you how He **IS** working in your life even when you can't see Him.

_____

_____

_____

_____

_____

_____

_____

_____

_____

_____

_____

_____

Looking For Peace

Philippians 4:6b
"Tell God what you need and thank Him for all He has done......." (NLT)

Christmastime is the season for singing songs like,

"Silent Night, Holy Night,"
and
"Peace on earth and mercy mild."

Christmas lights sparkle throughout our neighborhoods as well as inside our homes.

We can't deny there's something about the holiday season that causes us all to feel a sense of peace and joy in the midst of our hustle and bustle.

Many Christmas movies, even if they leave out the exact message of Jesus' birth, include characters coming together in church scenes at some point in the movie in order to experience the "feeling" of holiday love.

Christmas is an annual reminder that we're all longing for more in this world than we get on a normal day-to-day basis.

Christmas brings hope for a better life, a better way, a better purpose.

Nativity scenes appear on shelves throughout stores and homes serving as visual reminders of the love God demonstrated when He sent His Son to not only change our calendar and but also change our planet.

Whether we have accepted Him or not, He came.

And history changed.

Suddenly, the calendar started moving in another direction.

People accepted Him or they rejected Him.

And today, we are faced with the same decision.

With all of this emotional stirring in our hearts as we reflect on the significance of the holiday season, Christmas can be extremely painful when we are grieving.

Maybe your heart is aching from the loss of a loved one or you're lacking the funds to make someone's Christmas wish come true.

Maybe you're realizing that deep inside something is missing, and the gnawing sense of restlessness makes you uncomfortable.

All the touching songs, sparkling lights, and joys of Christmas can easily leave those of us who are grieving with a sense of emptiness and pain.

How can we find peace in the holiday season?

How can we become people who handle the good, the bad, the happy, and the sad with a sense of joy even when our heart is in anguish?

How can we keep on trusting that one day all things will be made right in His presence?

This morning, I was reading Philippians 4, and Paul's simple formula for peace seemed to jump off the page and affect me in a way it never had before.

Paul writes, "Tell God what you need, and thank Him for all He has done, then you will experience God's peace, which exceeds anything we can understand. His peace will guard your hearts and minds as you live in Christ Jesus."

If you find yourself feeling a sense of "peace-lessness" today, try doing these two things:

Tell God what you need
Thank Him for all He has done

See what happens as you turn to Him today with an honest and thankful heart.

REFLECTION TIME:

If you are like me, it is difficult to say "thank you" to God as you walk the road of grief. Take a few minutes, though, and try to list some things you are thankful for in spite of your heartache. How do you feel as you begin to praise Him even though your heart is broken?

_____

_____

_____

_____

_____

_____

_____

_____

_____

_____

_____

_____

FACING DAWN

Still Yelling, "Why?"

John 16:33
"I have told you these things, so that in me you may have peace. In this world you will have trouble. But take heart! I have overcome the world."

"Why????" one woman wailed as she ran down the road near the elementary school.
Uttering the only word that seemed to carry any meaning on that day, she screamed what we've all screamed in our minds over and over again since Friday as we've watched the story unfold like scenes from a nightmarish movie.
Why????
I'm sure God has listened to a lot of heart-wrenching cries since Friday morning.
I'm sure He's been leaned on, clung to, and cursed ever since the first shot was fired in a small, quiet town in Connecticut.
I'm sure He's heard longer and more complicated questions than simply, "Why?" since the day so many innocent lives were taken,
and I'm sure He's going to hear many, many more.

I don't think we'll find answers to the question, "Why?" while we're on this planet.
I don't think any amount of research or evidence will be enough to explain the events of Friday.
I definitely know that NOTHING investigators uncover will bring peace to the aching hearts of family members who have faced each morning since Friday with empty arms.

This tragedy has turned Christmas upside down all over the world.
It has caused many in Newtown to take down their decorations.

All I can say this morning is this,
God promises to be close to the brokenhearted.
He walks through the valley of the shadow of death with every single crushed heart in Newtown.
His presence in this small town today and tomorrow and the next day is as certain as the rising sun.
God is there.

The Creator of the universe, the Author of every story, the Redeemer of all mankind,
He is there.

We'll begin to hear stories as the weeks unfold.
We may have to dig deep and listen closely,
but we will begin to hear the stories of how God is speaking to the hurting in Newtown.

There are no words this morning that seem adequate.
There are no explanations that make sense.

But, in the midst of all of this confusion and chaos,
stirred by evil and by the one who comes to steal, kill, and destroy,
there is a Savior,
who offers peace in a troubled world.

Cling to Him today in your life's turmoil and questions.
Turn to Him today with your fears and doubts.
Answers can't always be found on an earthly level,
but God can be found at any level.

Look up with your questions,
and allow Him to be enough for your answer.

One day our faith will become sight.
One day perfection will overcome imperfection.
Until then, put your hope and trust in the One who will
overcome.

REFLECTION TIME:

Do you have questions about your grief? Do you feel uncertain about God's presence in your pain? Tell Him how you feel. Pour out every question on your mind. He longs to hear from you, even when your only question is "Why?" You may not find all your answers along the way; but if you turn the right direction in your search, you are certain to find Him. And in the end, He is always the right answer.

_____

_____

_____

_____

_____

_____

_____

_____

_____

_____

_____

_____

_____

_____

As Your Grief Unfolds

Psalm 34:18
The LORD is close to the brokenhearted and saves those
who are crushed in spirit.

I can barely believe we're starting our fifth year on this
planet without Nick.
Time has a way of marching forward regardless of our
unwillingness to see it pass.
I remember vividly the feelings I had early in my grief when
I didn't want to get to this place.....
this place where Christmas became less about who was
missing and more about who was present.
For a long time, I couldn't bear to look at Nick's pictures
without feeling overwhelming sadness.

Now I can look at his photographs and smile, remembering
fondly all the love and joy he brought and still brings to our
family.
I'm really not sure how this happened, and honestly,
part of me wants to fight it.
I never wanted to get use to Nick not being right around the
corner,
ready to surprise me or say something silly.
I never wanted to wake up and not feel that chest-crushing
agony as I remembered, once again, he was gone.

But, somehow, it's happened.

Our family laughs again.
Our family plays games again.
Our family celebrates again.
Our family dreams again.

As the mom in the midst of all of this adjusting and change, I
have to fight the urge to protest.
I have to fight the desire to stand up and say, "What about
Nick?!?!"

And, I have to keep going back to Him who understands me
more than anyone here ever could.
The One who gave His own Son up for me and patiently
watches me dive into life on this planet headstrong,
not always thinking about how His Son fits into my plans.....

I'm sure He fights the desire OFTEN to protest,
to somehow stand up and say,
"What about Jesus?"

I'm sure He watches my life unfold, smiling when the
unfolding reveals layers of me that have been wrapped in
moments with Him.
And I'm sure He works hard to be patient with all of the
unfolding of time that reveals layers of me wrapped in things
of much less significance.

As a new year begins, I'm thankful for four words that
remind me that even though my life and grief are constantly
changing, God never does.
While reading in my chronological Bible on January 1st,
I was struck with the first four words of Scripture,
"In the beginning, God..."

My desire for this year and for every new dawn is to keep
God in the beginning of all parts of my life.

I want every breath, every moment, every word to be
wrapped in Him.
No matter how much my life changes, I am thankful for one
constant assurance,
God is with me.

He is with you too.

REFLECTION TIME:

I don't know how long you've been walking the road of grief, but God knows, and He's been walking beside you all along the way. Have you invited Him into your grief, asking Him to face each new dawn with you? Today, I challenge you to write God a letter asking Him to join you on this painful road in a very intimate and personal way. Every day is a day for new beginnings. Choose today to face each new dawn with the One who began a good work in you long ago.

_____

_____

_____

_____

_____

_____

_____

_____

_____

_____

_____

_____

_____

Listening For Him

James 1:19
"My dear brothers and sisters, take note of this: Everyone should be quick to listen, slow to speak, and slow to become angry."

My word for this year is "Listen."

I want to talk less and listen more.

I want to be more aware of God's presence.

I want to know what He wants me to know and do what He wants me to do.

I was cleaning in my kitchen the other day after feeling very convicted by the Scripture in James that says, "Be quick to listen and slow to speak."

While cleaning and reflecting on this passage, I accidently knocked a figurine from my Nativity set off the windowsill above my kitchen sink.

I don't know why I was surprised when I picked up the figurine and realized that it was not only the most stubborn character in my Nativity scene but it was also now missing one ear!

God was already beginning to speak to me in a very loud voice as I picked up my little donkey and placed him back with his animal friends.

He was saying, "No matter how stubborn you might be, you **will** learn to listen this year."

So, I'm keeping my sweet little donkey right in front of me all year long..........as a reminder.

God wants me to be "quick to listen."

And He has plenty to say.

He longs to speak to you too.

REFLECTION TIME:
As you journey the painful road of grief, think about ways
God speaks to you. Maybe it's through nature. Maybe it's
through art or music. Maybe it's even through broken
Nativity figurines. Write about a couple of ways you will be
listening or watching for God to speak to you in the months
to come. Pray that He will show up in mighty ways as you
turn to Him for strength, peace, hope, and joy. Never forget
this verse, "The LORD is close to the brokenhearted and
saves those who are crushed in spirit." Psalm 34:18. When
someone is close to you, it is easier to hear him speak. Draw
close to Him today, tomorrow, and the next.
Listen to what He has to say to you.

_____

_____

_____

_____

_____

_____

_____

_____

_____

_____

_____

Please stay in touch with me by visiting

www.tammynischan.blogspot.com,

"My Heart His Words"

or by sending an email to

tammynischan@yahoo.com.

You are in my daily prayers.

Author Biography

Tammy Nischan is both a Proverbs 31 She Speaks and CLASS (Christian Leaders and Speakers) graduate whose mission is to empower the brokenhearted to find purpose and passion in their pain.

The mother of four children here on earth and two in Heaven, Tammy understands both the joys of parenthood and the heartache of losing a child. Twenty years ago, Tammy and her husband lost their six-week old daughter Adrienne to SIDS. Ten years later, they discovered that their youngest son, Nick, had a brain tumor. Caring for him for six years as he fought a long and courageous battle with brain cancer brought a new level of understanding to Tammy's heart as she experienced firsthand the fear and depression of a mom facing the nightmare of having a child who was terminally ill. Watching Nick lose his earthly battle and gain his Heavenly crown, Tammy was forced to walk the painful road of loss and grief all over again.

Tammy uses her years of experience as a minister's wife, educator, and children's minister combined with her countless moments as a mom to help women face life with a smile. Her sense of humor and ability to look at life through the eyes of God cause even the simplest moments in time to become life lessons.

Tammy has co-authored a children's book **Twenty Memory Verses Every Child Should Know**, been a contributing writer in **Hugs: Bible Reflections for Women**, and has had stories published in five recent editions of the **Chicken Soup for the Soul** series.

You can stay connected with Tammy by visiting her blog, *My Heart His Words*, at **www.tammynischan.blogspot.com** where she blogs almost daily as she strives to journey closer and closer to the heart of God in the midst of her heartache.

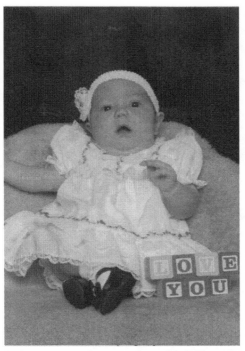

Adrienne Annabeth Nischan
3/15/92 – 4/30/92

*Our first daughter after two precious little boys, Adrienne
filled our hearts and home with bonnets and the color pink.
She captivated our hearts within seconds and we are forever
thankful for every kiss, every cuddle time, and every second
God allowed her to share life with us before the morning we
awoke to find she had died of SIDS. We'll never understand
why she was taken from us so unexpectedly on the morning of
Tim's birthday in 1992, but we cling to the promise that one
day all of our tears will be washed away forever and in an
instant our faith will become sight.*

Nicholas Yancy Nischan

5/22/95 – 11/29/08

Nick was diagnosed with his first brain tumor at the age of seven. Surgery, chemo, and radiation allowed him to have over four years of nearly normal life (attending school and participating on both the school basketball and football teams) after this diagnosis. At the age of 11, though, his cancer returned and the next 2 ½ years were filled with many surgeries, chemo and radiation treatments, transfusions, and hospital stays. On November 29, 2008, Nick was called Home. His smile never wavered as he fought cancer, and the memory of that smile keeps us going today. His bravery in the midst of painful situations still inspires us today, and we look forward with great faith to the day when our tears of grief are exchanged for songs of joy.

Zachary Charles Yoho

9/28/87 to 3/30/07

Zach was diagnosed with Type 1 diabetes just before his tenth birthday and with epilepsy just one week before having a fatal seizure. He graduated from West Liberty Salem High School where he was the Class VP his senior year. He was attending Free Will Baptist Bible College in Nashville, TN, when he passed away. He loved life and loved people. He was truly a gift from God and the joy of his parents' lives.